SAILOR ON SNOWSHOES

SAILOR ON SNOWSHOES

Tracking Jack London's Northern Trail

Dick North

HARBOUR PUBLISHING

Harbour Publishing Co. Ltd.
P.O. Box 219
Madeira Park, BC
V0N 2H0
www.harbourpublishing.com

Photographs by Dick North except where noted
Cover: Portrait of young Jack London courtesy Bancroft Library, University of California, Berkeley, 94720-6000 (image cropped, coloured and digitally enhanced)
Map on page ix by Roger Handling
Edited by Betty Keller
Design by Anna Comfort

Printed and bound in Canada

Harbour Publishing acknowledges financial support from the Government of Canada through the Book Publishing Industry Development Program and the Canada Council for the Arts, and from the Province of British Columbia through the British Columbia Arts Council and the Book Publisher's Tax Credit through the Ministry of Provincial Revenue.

BRITISH
COLUMBIA
ARTS COUNCIL

THE CANADA COUNCIL   LE CONSEIL DES ARTS
FOR THE ARTS   DU CANADA
SINCE 1957   DEPUIS 1957

Library and Archives Canada Cataloguing in Publication

North, Dick
  Sailor on snowshoes : tracking Jack London's northern trail / Dick North.

Includes bibliographical references and index.
ISBN 1-55017-384-7

  1. London, Jack, 1876-1916—Homes and haunts—Yukon Territory—Klondike River Valley. 2. Klondike River Valley (Yukon)—Gold discoveries. I. Title.

PS3523.O46Z783   2006   971.9'102'092   C2006-
900286-X

This book is dedicated to Pete Seibert who overcame terrible wounds suffered in Italy to build a wonderful life for himself and his family, and many others in Vail, Colorado.

CONTENTS

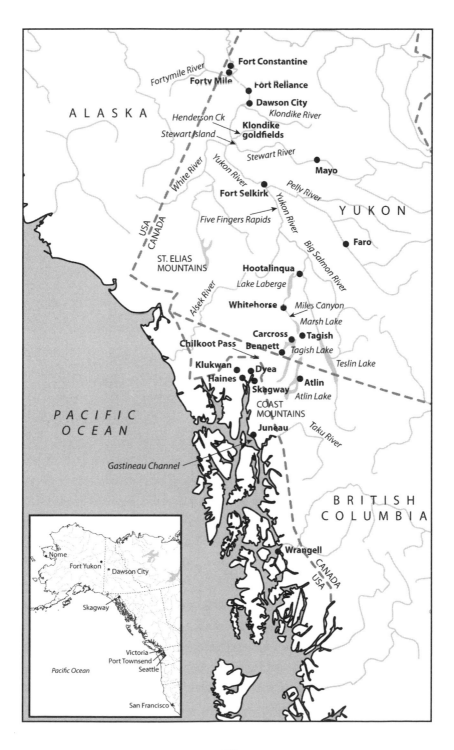

ACKNOWLEDGEMENTS

Alan Innes-Taylor and Holly Macdonald were indispensable in obtaining the permission of the Yukon Historical Sites Board with regards to moving the Jack London cabin out of the wilderness. The members of the board were very helpful: Jack Andison, Victoria Faulkner, C.H. Chapman, Reverend Ken Snider and Laurent Cyr.

Without the aid and support of Commissioner James Smith, his assistant Frank Fingland and Jack Gibson, director of the Travel and Publicity Department for the Yukon Territory, the project would never have come to a successful conclusion. The same applies for their counterparts in Oakland, California— Ben Nutter, manager of the Port Authority of Oakland; Robert Mortensen, president of the Board of Directors of the Port; and Boots Erb, president of the Jack London Square Merchants' Association.

Eddie Albert's participation enhanced the project and gave a big boost to the general concept of restoration of historical sites.

Thanks are in order for James Mellor, former mayor of Dawson City who, along with city council, was responsible for the wonderful reception afforded the Oakland group.

Gary Trew and "Mac" Munroe of the Mining Recorder's Office of Dawson City were of great help to my research of the claims filed by London and his friends of 1897–98.

John Gould of Dawson City did an excellent job of photographing claim applications on file in the Mining Recorder's Office, thus providing invaluable copies for my use.

Hensley Woodbridge, co-author of the one complete bibliography of Jack London's works, was of great help in supplying references in regard to London's activity in the Klondike.

King Hendricks of Utah State University graciously allowed me to read several original documents of London's including the never-before-published (at that time) "A Clondyke Christmas" and Fred Thompson's diary.

Irving Shepard gave me several original cheques signed by London to compare with the handwriting found in the cabin. His son Milo presented me with the volumes of London's short stories and letters.

Joan London Miller, Jack London's eldest daughter, was of considerable aid in my search for stories of her father, as was London's second daughter Bess Fleming in relation to the dedication of the Oakland cabin.

Don Schmiege of the US Forest Service introduced me to Gus Wahlgren (via the mails). Wahlgren tree-ring dated the logs of the cabin at the Forest Products Lab of the US Forest Service in Madison, Wisconsin; Pat Lister of Whitehorse bundled up the log cross sections for mailing.

Document examiners Ludlow Baynard of Baton Rouge, Louisiana, and Donald Doud of Milwaukee, Wisconsin, are to be thanked for giving their time to the project, as are examiners with the Royal Canadian Mounted Police in Ottawa, Ontario, and Edmonton, Alberta.

Rose Wood Zeniuk's help in locating the signature slab and Gordon MacIntyre's photos of it were much appreciated. Also of help were Rose's daughter and son-in-law, Maggie and Dick Wallingham.

To the guides, Joe Henry, and his crew of his son Victor and John Semple, and to the cook Eleanor Millard, I extend my thanks for jobs well done.

The Yukon Archives and Libraries were indispensable.

Charlie Benson of Whitehorse was responsible for getting

the truck in running condition in order to carry the Oakland-bound cabin to California.

Roy McDiarmid donated the services of his Klondike Express truck to move the cabin from Dawson City to Whitehorse, YT, and Diane Murphy and Mike Miller of the Alaska Department of Travel, provided transportation for the truck and cabin from Haines, Alaska, to Seattle, Washington.

Special credits are in order for John Reading, mayor of Oakland, who graciously made the trip for the dedication of the London cabin in Dawson City on August 17, 1969, and to Rev. Ken Snider, who has been a continuing participant in making the Dawson City monument a success. I extend appreciation to Nancy Campbell of Oakland for introductions and transportation she afforded our team while we were in that city.

The news media helped considerably. This included the *Klondike Korner,* published in Dawson City, the *Whitehorse Star*, the *Juneau Empire, Oakland Tribune, Oakland Times, Fairbanks News-Miner*, Associated Press, Canadian Press, Canadian Broadcasting Company and the one hundred television stations that displayed the film clip of the 1969 expedition.

The advertising firm Wyckoff and Associates was of great help.

Special consideration goes to Ken Shortt, former publisher of the *Yukon Daily News,* for his constant support during my years of research. The same goes for John Keating, who was president of the Yukon Historical Society, and to Henk Wijnen, publisher of the *Midnight Sun.*

John Nielsen, employee of the Arkansas State Park Service and later Alaska, was helpful in supplying additional photos from his trip into the cabin site in the fall of 1965.

John Boston of the RCMP, Geoffrey Simmonds of Utah State University Archives, Milo Shepard, now executor for the London estate, Bruce Harvey of Canada's Historic Sites

Department and Alan Jutzi of the Huntington Library rendered invaluable assistance when it was needed.

Ron Ryant at TastyByte Internet Cafe was a great help with email correspondence.

Above all, credit should go to Russ Kingman of Glen Ellen, California; Roy Minter, formerly of the White Pass and Yukon Route; and to Rudy, Yvonne, Robin, Linda and Ivan Burian. If it had not been for their interest and participation, there never would have been a project.

Credit goes to the lads who put the sod roof on the Dawson City cabin and should not be forgotten—Peter and John Snider, Vince Fraser, the Anderson brothers, Gary Langevin, and to the man who helped the Burians put up the Dawson City cabin, Willie De Wolfe.

And of course, thanks go to my wife Andrée, who has always been my sounding board, confidante and chief critic.

And lastly, thanks to Mrs. Tom Firth for her continuing support and interest with respect to the creation and building of the Jack London Interpretive Centre in Dawson City. Credit should also go to the Klondike Visitors Association and the territorial and federal governments for their assistance. The many individuals who helped on that project are listed in the exhibit itself along with a photo taken on the day of dedication.

FOREWORD

In 1913 in his semi-autobiographical book *John Barleycorn* Jack London wrote, "I brought nothing back from the Klondike but my scurvy." He knew better than this, of course. He brought only a few dollars in gold dust home from the Klondike, but he brought home something infinitely more precious: the raw material for a spectacular career that has no parallel in the history of American literature. To the end of his life he mined his northland experiences; indeed, a strong argument can be made that London's greatest literary works are the product of the year (August 1897 to July 1898) he spent in the Yukon Territory. "There," he said a few years after he returned home to San Francisco, "I found myself. There nobody talks. Everybody thinks. You get your true perspective. I got mine."

Dick North got his perspective there, too.

In his Introduction to this book he says of London, "If our maker was going to prescribe an individual to romanticize the Klondike gold rush, he could have found no one more qualified."

I maintain that the same could be said of North: no better individual could have been selected by maker or mortal to find Jack London's gold-rush cabin and romanticize its occupant's history.

For the first thirty-four years of his life, North would seem an unlikely candidate to follow London's footsteps into the Yukon. Born in New Jersey, raised in Long Island and West Virginia, and educated in New Hampshire, North ventured to California after service in Italy in World War II and after earning a degree at George Washington University. He earned a BA degree at the University of California at Berkeley in 1954, and rattled around in miscellaneous employment for a decade until a reporting job with the *Las Vegas Review Journal* sent him to Alaska and sealed his fate and future as a man of the north country.

He may have had some exposure to Jack London in a UC literature course or even in his days at GWU in Washington, but as he relates in this book, he made a real, lifelong connection as a senior at UC when he dropped in at the First and Last Chance Saloon in Oakland—London's favourite hangout in his early-1890s oyster-pirating days. Whatever the case, it seems inevitable that North would drift into Yukon Territory, the place that inspired his literary mentor, and there make a name for himself as a newspaperman and book writer.

Dick North loves a mystery and has made memorable books of the mysteries he has found in the Canadian northlands. In *The Mad Trapper of Rat River* (1972), for example, he undertook to tell the story of the solitary trapper who in the winter of 1931–32 shot an officer of the RCMP and fled into the Yukon wilderness along the Arctic Circle. This man, whose identity North assiduously uncovered, survived four armed encounters with the Mounties, as they pursued him for two months and 150 miles on foot and by dogsled in minus-forty-degree weather to a fatal showdown. In *The Lost Patrol* (1978), he traced in meticulous detail one of the most poignant tragedies of the RCMP: the death in 1911 of Inspector Francis J. Fitzgerald and three other Mounties while on a gruelling dogsled patrol out of Fort McPherson, NWT.

All of his books are eloquently written but a particularly poetic passage from *The Lost Patrol*, eerily reminiscent of such Jack London story classics as "To the Man on Trail" and "The White Silence," proves that North is a true "Son of the Wolf," a writer deserving of Jack London brotherhood and the perfect person to write *Sailor on Snowshoes*.

"The magnetism of trail life in the North is made up of many things," North wrote in *The Lost Patrol*:

> It is the crack of a spruce tree splitting in the frigid temperature. It is the flickering of candlelight that cheerily illuminates a canvas shelter. It is the startling flutter of wings when a flock of ptarmigan rise from an approaching dog team. It is the silent dance of the multicoloured aurora as it flits across the skies. It is the physical exhilaration of meeting each day's challenge and mastering it. It is the wholesome smell of caribou steak sizzling in a frying pan and setting the saliva to flow. It is the crunch of snowshoes and the rasp of a toboggan as it grates across an ice hummock. It is the comic gurgle of the raven as he hops into camp looking for a handout. It is the sibilant sound of ice expanding and contracting on a nearby creek. It is the fragrant aroma of spruce boughs that permeates the tent at night. It is the sight of a band of caribou wandering spectrelike in the morning mists. It is the camaraderie of men helping one another to achieve a common goal. It is the refreshing freedom of the trail.

In *Sailor on Snowshoes* North not only solves the mystery of the whereabouts of the cabin that London occupied in the fall and winter of 1897, but traces to the Yukon settlement of Mayo a slab of wood from the cabin on which London wrote his name and identified himself as "miner, author." In addition, he gives a succinct recounting of London's gold rush year in the Yukon, telling of the friends who accompanied him and those he met on the trail from Chilkoot Pass to Dawson City. The author even introduces a new mystery: a possible photographic image of London taken at Sheep Camp on the Chilkoot trail in September 1897 by pioneer cameraman, Frank LaRoche.

I have admired Dick North's work for many years and closely followed the story of his discovery of the London cabin when it began to unfold in the early '60s. I am delighted to see that adventure, and a lively new recounting of London's critical year in the Yukon, in this splendid book.

—Dale L. Walker, January 11, 2006

Dale L. Walker is the Texas-based author of twenty books of history and biography. He has a lifelong interest in Jack London and has written extensively about the author in such book-length studies as *Jack London and Conan Doyle: A Literary Kinship* (1981), *Curious Fragments: Jack London's Tales of Fantasy Fiction* (1975), and *No Mentor But Myself: Jack London, the Writer's Writer* (1999).

INTRODUCTION

The Klondike gold rush was not a choice destination for anyone without strength or moral resolve, and no one was to come along as a better champion for this century-ending epic than a twenty-one-year-old unemployed lad from California named Jack London. If our maker was going to prescribe an individual to romanticize the Klondike gold rush, he could have found no one more qualified. A deep-sea sailor with ten years of small-craft experience on San Francisco Bay, he could sail anything under forty feet. The eddies and air currents of the vast sound posed no problems for him, night or day, a fact that would stand well for him on the lakes and waterways of the Yukon. At five feet seven inches in height, he weighed a muscular 160 pounds and had unusually wide shoulders, as if they had been carved for the purpose of carrying a pack full of supplies across the dreaded notch known as Chilkoot Pass.

His life prior to the gold rush had been a story of lean days cooking over outdoor fires and making do with everything from mulligan stew of the hobo jungles to fish freshly caught from the waters of the Sacramento River. He knew how to pitch a tent and to start a fire with minimal effort, but could get by with neither if he had to. He had lived in close quarters with sailors before the mast, with tramps on the road, and after the time he was picked up for vagrancy, with convicts in jail.

Although London had not sold a story yet, he had pursued the proper preparation of untold numbers of words written, studied and hacked out in his efforts to become a writer. He had won a newspaper competition wherein his description of a typhoon off the coast of Japan, experienced when he was a sailor,

Gold rush photographer Frank LaRoche captured the only picture that
has ever surfaced of Jack London (centre) in the Klondike. *University of
Washington Libraries, Special Collections, LaRoche 2033 (cropped)*

was good enough to beat out scores of writers with more education than he had. His stories revealed a man who was sensitive yet outgoing and humorous. Jack London had the right stuff to prevail through a winter with rough-hewn prospectors in a tiny far-north cabin.

He set sail for the Klondike to accumulate gold rather than to write about it, but lurking in the back of his mind he always maintained a resolve to become a novelist. Everywhere he wandered, his alert intellect absorbed the ingredients he would later organize into the mesmerizing stories that remain to this day the finest record of the gold rush. He has brought to the reader, as few other authors have done, the feeling, the atmosphere, the conversations, the power of the cold, the sense of urgency, the romance and the stark reality of survival in the wilderness.

Sailor on Snowshoes is, therefore, a wilderness ramble through Jack London's gold rush to find and preserve its tangible relics. In particular, it is the story of the search for a Yukon bush cabin in which London wrote his name. The author hopes this tale will not only afford a deeper insight into London as a young man, and the far-off land that inspired his fame, but also present the rudiments of on-the-scene research and the painstaking steps of restoration and preservation.

1: FLASHBACK

Robin Burian was making fourteen knots in his freight canoe as we proceeded up the Yukon River toward his home on Stewart Island, some seventy-five miles south of Dawson City. It was May 12, 1969, and the twenty-six-year-old trapper was taking me to view the restoration work in which he was engaged. The Yukon River breakup was still in progress, as was evident by the ice floes that flashed past us on the swift current.

"I had to pick my way through ice jams coming down," Robin said, "and they looked like they were ready to go any minute."

We veered right and left to avoid the floes that descended upon us as we fought our way up the waterway with the help of Robin's powerful 18-hp outboard. We were perhaps a mile below the junction where Jim Creek meets the Yukon River when an ice jam above us let go with a roar. A swirling mass of ice, logs and water rose above the river like a tidal wave and then burst out, rushing toward us at ten knots. In seconds the first cakes rattled our vulnerable craft like a swizzle stick in a gin on the rocks.

I did my best to fend off several of the giant ice cubes with my paddle while Robin swung the craft and poured on full power in a desperate effort to reach the sanctuary of a sandbar to our right. Then a ten-ton ice cake caromed off the right bank of the river, spinning like a top and threatening to crush our fragile boat against another ice block that loomed in front of us. Had we used a shoehorn, we could not have squeezed any closer between these two frosty nutcrackers. We had mere inches to spare. Though it was cold on the river, I found myself drenched in sweat when we reached the sandbar.

It's only when you undergo an adventure like this that you really comprehend the genius of the individual who wrote regularly about such events—Jack London. In his short story "Rainbow's End," he tells of a character named Donald and his companions who are trapped on an island by rising water caused by the backup from an ice jam on the Yukon River. Donald has climbed a tree to escape the water and to check on another jam forming upriver. He realizes if it breaks before the lower jam gives way, it will be curtains for him and his comrades:

> ...and now his voice rang out, "God Almighty, here she comes!"
>
> Standing knee-deep in the icy water, the Minook men, with Montana Kid and the policeman, gripped hands and raised voices in the terrible "Battle Hymn of the Republic." But the words were drowned in the advancing roar.
>
> And to Donald was vouchsafed a sight such as no man may see and live. A great wall of white flung itself upon the island. Trees, dogs, men were blotted out, as though the hand of God had wiped the face of nature clean. This much he saw, then swayed an instant longer in his lofty perch and hurtled far out into the frozen hell.

Obviously, my own brush with the ice jam could have been worse. But what made that adventure in May 1969 significant for me was that it had been launched some fifteen years earlier during an afternoon spent in Jack London's old hangout, the First and Last Chance Saloon in Oakland, California. At the time, the University of California at nearby Berkeley was adjudicating my efforts as a senior transfer student, and the atmosphere of the little bar had provided a welcome break from my studies.

On that particular day the proprietor of the First and Last Chance, George Heinold, had held me spellbound at the canted bar in his lopsided bistro while the base refrain of ships' bellows provided a resonant background. San Francisco Bay, whose grey waters lapped at the bulkheads of the inner harbour less than a block away, impregnated the atmosphere with the smack of creosote, iodine, salt and seaweed. The building had originally been a bunkhouse for oyster pirates with whom London had chummed as a teenager, but Heinold's father, John, had converted it into a saloon in the mid-1880s. The 1906 earthquake dealt it a savage blow, knocking it into a north-south slant, but it failed to put the pub out of business, and Heinold had continued to operate it in its rearranged state. Ironically, it was one of the books London was to partially write in the First and Last Chance that eventually served to close the establishment. This was his famous indictment of alcohol, *John Barleycorn*, which became a bestseller and was used as a tool by prohibitionists to push the Eighteenth Amendment through the United States Congress. This action shut down all the saloons in the country four years after London's 1916 death, but John Heinold had adjusted by operating the bistro as a sandwich shop for the next fifteen years.

John Heinold had passed away twenty-one years before I visited the saloon in 1954, and by that time his son had become the epitome of the professional proprietor-bartender. Whether the subject was the latest sports score or a customer's personal problems, he could be counted on to supply an eclectic empathy. This friendliness was also apparent in his employees, including that white-haired purveyor of beverages, Bill Tilley. There seldom was a day when the customer was not a king. However, George and his employees were not without a sense of humour and never missed an opportunity to tease their customers. This included installing a loudspeaker in the unisex restroom, over which the bartenders would often excitedly vocalize to the consternation of the customer who happened to be in there.

Now Heinold, his broad forehead in a seemingly perpetual frown, was delivering a talk about Jack London, who had been a personal friend to him and his father. Visitors loved Heinold's storytelling, and except for a few embellishments his account was reasonably accurate. "Jack London wrote his bestselling novels *John Barleycorn* and *The Sea Wolf* right at that table you are sitting at," he declared, pointing to the group of tourists nearest him. He was stretching the truth somewhat. If he had said "parts of the books," he would have been more correct, but who was going to quibble over a minor point like that? How many saloons ever served a habitual customer who was a novelist, and how many more could boast his books numbered half a million in print in over fifty languages a full thirty-eight years after his death?

While Heinold continued, my eyes drifted over the innards of the saloon. Its walls were covered with a jumble of artifacts ranging from souvenirs of the great earthquake of 1906 to more contemporary mementos. The conglomeration included a sea captain's hat slung loosely from a nail, a sheriff's well-worn star, withered old letters and envelopes, autographed currency of World War II vintage, several anachronous calendars, a World War I helmet suspended from the ceiling by its chin strap from which German military decorations hung in profusion. These were probably "captured" by George, who won a bevy of his own medals during his stint with an American Marine brigade attached to the US Second Infantry Division at the Battle of Marne. Assorted archaeological debris, including thousands of business cards, were strewn helter-skelter on the ceiling and walls. But the featured nook of the bistro was to the left as one walked through the door. Protected by a brace of chicken wire, this cranny incorporated assorted memorabilia of Jack London, who had authored fifty books in the eighteen years between his return from the Klondike in far-off Canada in 1898 and his death at forty years of age in 1916. Crammed behind the wire was a likeness of the brown-haired, blue-eyed author, a portrait of his favourite black stallion and other dust-covered rubble attesting to the great man's past.

As I listened to George Heinold, it was like looking through a window into the past. As a child, he recalled London holding him on his knee while recounting his adventures in the Klondike, Korea, Japan and the sealing islands of the northern Pacific. London would talk for a spell, then set the boy down and pick up a scratch pen to continue with his writing. Heinold then went on to describe the impact of his famous bar on the author's career. It seems that John Heinold had put up the money for London to attend the University of California at Berkeley in the fall of 1896. He had also been the source of encouragement when London was struggling to make a living as a writer and others were berating him for taking up an occupation at which he was so unlikely to succeed. But the tavern owner was a man of acute perception. In an interview shortly before his death in 1933, he had recalled not London's drinking but his interest in the huge dictionary that was kept in the saloon. At fifteen, he said, London would take the book to a table near the door and study it by the hour, oblivious to the noise around him. The proprietor saw in this the same totality of effort London would later demonstrate in just about every project he undertook; this youth not only possessed the talent to master new words but also had the perseverance and dedication needed to weave them into readable material.

Jack London's books had always piqued my interest. His dog stories *The Call of the Wild* and *White Fang* and the short but gripping yarn of a man who freezes to death on a Yukon trail, "To Build a Fire," had instilled in me an underlying desire to go where the action took place. Even as a youngster, I had longed to be where the vast untrodden forests teemed with wolves, moose, grizzlies and caribou. And I wondered, could there be a cabin standing somewhere in the northern wilds in which London had once lived? If so and if the cabin could be proved as such, this would be equivalent to finding a lost treasure!

George Heinold, proprietor-bartender of the First and Last Chance Saloon.

When George Heinold finished his stories, I solicited his thoughts on the subject of a cabin.

He drew a beer and passed it to the tourist sitting next to me before he said, "I don't know why there wouldn't be."

Playing the devil's advocate, I argued that fifty-seven years or so was a long time for such a structure to survive.

"How long do you think *this* shack has been here?" he asked.

I shrugged.

"Over sixty years," he countered.

"But your place is different. This is a warmer climate, and it's been lived in."

He shook his head. "We have wet winters. Dampness makes wood rot. It's dryer in the north."

Referring to Irving Stone's popular biography of London, *Sailor on Horseback,* I countered, "Stone wrote that Jack and a friend dismantled the cabin they were living in at a place called Stewart Island. They made a raft out of it, floated downriver to Dawson City and sold the raft for the wood in it. This being the case, there would be no cabin to resurrect!"

The background noise had abated as the bar's clientele listened to us, half-hypnotized—which did not hurt Heinold's sense of the dramatic. He eyed all of us before he spoke. "Sure," he said, "but the cabin you mention was right next to the Yukon River. I remember Jack telling me that he lived in more than one cabin when he was up there."

So maybe there was such a cabin in existence.

On rereading Stone's book in my tiny apartment in Berkeley that night, I realized that the closest London ever came to residing permanently anywhere in the north was at Stewart Island. This fronted on the Yukon River between the mouths of the Stewart River and Henderson Creek, and according to Stone, London had staked a gold claim on Henderson Creek. The next day, in order to better pinpoint the author's journeys, I went to the university library and took out Charmian London's biography of her husband, *The Book of Jack London*. Her account included dates provided by a diary loaned to her by Fred Thompson, who had accompanied London on his trip to the Klondike; this confirmed his itinerant status. The only place he had lived for any length of time besides Stewart Island was Dawson City, where he had remained for two months in the fall and three weeks the following spring. During the former period he lived in a tent and during the latter his station was unknown. He departed Dawson City in June 1898, sailing down the Yukon River by boat. He reached the Bering Sea at the end of the month and immediately caught a ship back to California.

These undisputed facts simplified my research. The only places he could have lived in a cabin were Dawson City, Stewart Island and Henderson Creek. Maps in the university library showed me that Stewart Island was about 275 miles north of Whitehorse and there were no roads to it. One would have to fly or take a boat. A dot on the map signified a hamlet where there might be a few residents who could possibly answer some questions about a shack.

Idle conversations in saloons have launched far weightier schemes than mine, and that day I resolved that, if ever the chance presented itself, I would look for such a cabin. The seed of interest had been planted, and it remained for the fates to decide whether an opportunity to harvest the results would ever arise.

2: HEADING NORTH

Ajob on New York's Wall Street beckoned me after graduation, but the huge city library quickly became my favourite hangout because it was filled with magazines, newspapers, and books published at the turn of the century. In the meantime, rereading *The Call of the Wild* helped put my interest in London's Yukon cabin into perspective because, incredibly, a cabin is an integral part of the book's plot. In the final chapter a log shack signifying the presence of a lost gold mine sits idle at the headwaters of the Stewart River. Searching for it, the central characters find gold but not the cabin.

After that, thumbing through other stories and articles by London revealed cabins as a recurring theme in his writings about the north. In a short story entitled "In a Far County," the turning point for the protagonists comes when the temperature and the blackness of the Arctic night bottom out in December. From then on the descent into the ultimate hell of despair—cabin fever—is swift and sure. He writes: "The intense frost could not be endured for long at a time, and the little cabin crowded them—beds, stove, table and all—into a space ten by twelve." The setting for this story was far up the Porcupine River where admittedly London had never journeyed, but I asked myself if he could have been envisioning another tiny structure in a place about which he was more familiar.

While in New York I hedged against the future by writing freelance material for the *Territorial Enterprise* of Virginia City, Nevada, the same newspaper that had hired Mark Twain a hundred years earlier. The *Enterprise* published two of my columns—"Snake Eyes," a humorous history of Nevada, and "Nevada Con Norte," a hodgepodge of vignettes on characters it had been my good fortune to have met or read about while prospecting for uranium in the Nevada desert. And when the lure of the west once again became too great to resist, these columns helped me land a job as editor of the Las Vegas *Review Journal's* editorial page.

Two months in that position went by quickly, then one day the editor, Bob Brown, approached with a proposal. "One of our reporters just up and quit on the *Daily Alaska Empire* in Juneau," he said. "How would you like to take his place?" Though aware that the *Empire,* like the *Review Journal,* was one of the newspapers owned by the Donrey Corporation of Las Vegas, I had not really connected them until Bob made his offer. After deliberating a polite thirty seconds, I signed on, and the next day I was on a flight to Juneau by way of Seattle.

Glimpsing Juneau as we passed over it for the swing into the airport, which was another ten miles to the east, I could see why Alaska's capital was called the San Francisco of the north. Like the Golden Gate city, Juneau was almost entirely clustered on hills, its homes lining the mountainsides bordering Gastineau Channel like so many wasps' nests plastered on an abandoned barn. The people here could step out of their front doors and find themselves on someone else's roof. Easily visible above the capital, sitting up there like a bowl of ice cream, was the gigantic Juneau ice field, the source of scores of glaciers that calved from it. It was this giant collection of ice that was also the origin—by way of the water emerging from it—of the mighty Yukon River. Westward lay Douglas Island, its shores constituting the west bank of Gastineau Channel. As the plane landed, the Mendenhall Glacier loomed above us like a huge blue-green comber poised to crash down on the matchbox-like houses that cluttered the valley to our right. When I stepped down from the plane, the magnitude of the glacier framing the eastern horizon was a first impression I could never forget.

Easing into my new home in this picturesque city was comparatively simple, though I soon found that my assignment to cover the state legislature was very intense and took a lot of time. Alaska had only achieved statehood four years earlier in 1959, and as a result the legislature was a very busy place. But my interest in Jack London was not forgotten, and I checked the state library to learn whether there were any previously unearthed documents about him that were gathering dust; the archivists assured me that there was nothing except a few novels in "general distribution."

While this news was disappointing, I soon discovered that my assignments as a reporter would take me to locales he had frequented or written about. One of those occasions came shortly after my arrival when red-thatched Jerry Shelley, an officer for the state's Department of Fish and Game, invited me to go on a fisheries patrol. This journey commenced in a skiff, but soon a radio call ordered us to anchor the boat in a slough off Lynn Canal and wait for a Grumman amphibian to pick us up. Our new destination was Elfin Cove, a picturesque little community nestled on Chichagof Island, near the lower end of Lynn Canal and not far from the actual scene of one of London's more grizzly tales. Our chore there was to catch fish pirates, but by the time we arrived they had disappeared. However, the journey was memorable just the same.

After the plane let us off at the cove's outer dock, we climbed a path that led to a small rise about fifty feet above the tidal level, and from this spot my eyes took in the beauty of Elfin Cove for the first time. The lagoon was egg-shaped, with its narrow entrance so well camouflaged by spruce and hemlock it could easily be missed at first glance. Though an endlessly thick, dark green forest loomed solemnly in every direction from the cove, a single row of alabaster houses hugged the foot of the hill bordering the lagoon, all of them fronting on a boardwalk just above the tidal drift. It served as Elfin Cove's one main street. Within the womb of the cove and tied to the dock were boats of all descriptions—gillnetters with their decks wallowing in mesh; ponderous purse seiners, their booms askew; trollers that looked like floating pin cushions with many poles protruding in all directions; pretentious yachts; and next to them, diminutive skiffs weighed down by oversized outboard motors.

The bespectacled, heavy-set local fish buyer, Gil Bixby, put Shelley and me up for the night in the comfortable house he shared with his wife and daughters. Bixby's service was a crucial one for the fishermen who cruised the area; by purchasing their fish, he saved some of them a long journey into Juneau.

The next morning at breakfast we were visited by Ernie Swanson, a lean Scandinavian who owned the general store. According to Bixby, Swanson's place was also the city hall, information and tourist bureau, post office and rumour mill. And when he introduced Shelley and myself, he pointed out that Swanson was also the founder of Elfin Cove. However, Swanson dismissed the claim with a wave of his hand. "I didn't build the first structure here," he said. "Sam Butts should get credit. He put up a small dock and warehouse here in 1928."

"But you blocked out the first home here, didn't you?" Bixby asked.

Swanson nodded. "That's true. Actually, the first man to

frequent the area was a fish buyer named Hutchison. He arrived with two boats, *The Resolute* and *The Comet* in 1927. He mild-cured fish here. The anchorage at that time was called the Gunk Hole."

I asked him about the name Elfin Cove.

"Named it after my boat," he said. "Gunk Hole didn't seem to fit a place like this."

While on the subject of history, I asked if he had ever heard of a man Jack London had written about, a man who was hanged over on the coast.

Swanson's lean Nordic face took on a grim look. "Who hasn't heard about it would be a better question," he said. "That happened over in Lituya Bay around the turn of the century."

"You been there?"

Swanson nodded. "When you see how difficult it is to get into Lituya Bay, you know the reason they went on their own and hanged the guy."

"How's that?"

"The entrance is shallow. You have to catch a high tide, and you don't have a lot of room for error. The locals couldn't flag down any passing ships to help them with this guy, who happened to have murdered a few people, so they went ahead with a solution of their own. That's what made the headlines."

"Cabin fever on the part of the hombre they hanged, Ernie?" Bixby asked.

"Could be. It does do funny things to people," Swanson replied. "Look at our neighbour, Chuck Harborson."

"Nice guy," said Bixby.

"Yes, but different than the rest of us," Swanson added, then explained, "He rows his boat over to my store for supplies about once every six months. He stays and talks with Gil and me, and then heads back to Dundas Bay. It's within the boundaries of Glacier Bay Park, but Chuck has 'grandfather rights' and the parks people can't kick him out. They have to wait until he dies or moves."

"He rows over here?" I asked.

Swanson nodded. "Yeah. Must be ten, twenty miles."

"Get rough?"

"The place is littered with sunken ships," Bixby injected.

Swanson paused to accept a cup of coffee from one of Bixby's daughters before continuing. "Gil and I are about the only ones he'll talk with. Even at his own cabin he makes himself scarce if someone shows up."

"How come?" I asked.

"He just doesn't want to jaw with anyone unless he has to."

"Then he's really a true hermit?"

"I'll say," Bixby chimed in. "A pilot dropped him some magazines one day. Several months later the pilot, who prided himself on his philanthropy, met the old guy at Ernie's store and asked if he'd enjoyed the magazines. Do you know what Chuck said? 'No. I don't want any magazines.'"

"I wonder what makes a guy that way?"

"It's hard telling," Swanson commented. "Cabin fever. Living alone. You name it. A long time ago Chuck worked in Juneau. Maybe he just got sick of civilization."

"How long has he lived at Dundas Bay?"

"About thirty years," said Swanson.

(Eight months after that visit to Elfin Cove, Chuck Harborson died alone in his cabin. It was cancer. His last words were found in a note he had left for the Bixbys. It said: "My guts are giving me hell." In his will the old hermit left several jars of salmonberry jam to the Bixby children.)

As we lifted off for the flight back to Juneau, the visibility was excellent, and we could see Cape Spencer in the distance. I knew that only a few score miles north of it lay Lituya Bay. Jack London's fiction piece "The Unexpected," about the event that occurred there, had stirred up a controversy in the literary world, with London himself at the centre of it. Published by *McClure's Magazine* in August 1905, his story tells of a blood-bath that took place among a party of gold miners a hundred miles north of Lituya Bay. Two men are murdered with a shotgun by a third man. Two survivors, a man and his wife, successfully subdue the gun wielder only to find that the burden of looking after him becomes unbearable. Ultimately, the couple, having no access to the courts, hold a trial of their own, convict the offender of murder and hang him.

Critics accused London of inventing an implausibly violent theme in order to wrench a few more dollars out of the coffers of the magazine publishers. One of these critics was the editor of the *Seattle Post-Intelligencer,* who scoffed at the assertion that the tale was based on fact, and he ripped apart both London and the story. London's response was a letter to the editor informing him he had read of the event in the *San Francisco Examiner,* datelined October 14, 1900, and suggesting the editor should lambaste the reporters on the *Examiner* and not him if the account was untrue.

In the Juneau archives I discovered a news item in the *Sitka Alaskan* of May 12, 1900. It read as follows: "The *Excelsior* reports a lynching bee at Lituya Bay. Two men were murdered there last fall, and it having been impossible to communicate with authorities at Sitka and fearing to set the murderer at large in the community, being satisfied of his guilt, the Lituyans thought it proper to take the law into their own hands, hence the elevation of the criminal."

I also found a news article published in the *Alaskan* on October 13, 1906. Though it verified London's story, there were some minor differences. Only one man was killed in the actual account, not two, and London had fictionalized some of the names. The victim's real name was Fragnallia Stefano, not

Harkey as in the story. Another man, Sam Christianson, was wounded whereas in the author's tale his name was Dutchy and he too was killed. According to the *Alaskan*, Sam Christianson was a well-known teamster in Juneau, and he reported the murderer's name to be M.S. Severts, not Michael Dennin as in London's yarn. The couple who survived the attack were Hans Nelson and Hannah Butler Nelson, and not Edith Whitelsey Nelson as London had written.

Christianson's account, however, was almost as gruesome as London's fiction. He said he, the Nelsons, Stefano and Severts were having dinner together on the evening of October 6, 1899. The conversation was pleasant with no arguments or discord to indicate what was going to happen. Severts finished dinner earlier than the others and went outside, returning moments later with a Colt .45 revolver in hand. He aimed the gun at Stefano and pulled the trigger, killing him instantly. Then without a word, Severts turned the gun on Christianson and fired. Incredibly, the slug hit a stone jar on the table and ricocheted into the back of the teamster's neck. Stunned, Christianson fell to the floor.

Severts then levelled his gun at Mrs. Nelson, but as he was about to pull the trigger, her husband leapt at the assassin, grabbing his gun-arm in a vice-like grip and jerking it downward. The pistol discharged into the killer's leg, creating an ugly wound. Meanwhile, Hannah had grabbed a towel, jumped at Severts, and wrapped the towel around his neck in a chokehold. The combined efforts of the Nelsons overcame the offender, but once this was accomplished and the man was tied up, they found themselves in the paradoxical situation of having to care for him. They treated his leg wound, then hired some Tlingit Indians to carry him four miles down the bay to a lower cabin, where they guarded him for several weeks.

After every effort had been made by the residents of Lituya

Lacking access to the courts, Hannah and Hans Nelson held trial and hanged the man who tried to murder them, inspiring London's short story "The Unexpected." *Atlin Museum*

Bay to flag a passing ship, the Nelsons held a trial (albeit unlawful in the eyes of the territorial government of Alaska) at which Severts acknowledged his guilt to them. When asked why he did it, he was noncommittal, but when it was suggested he killed for the eight hundred dollars in gold his associates had accumulated, he said, "Maybe." Later he signed a confession to that effect, admitting his plan was to blame the murder on the Native people. The Nelsons then proceeded to hang him.

Hans and Hannah Nelson were placed on probation and were required to report periodically by mail to the Juneau authorities. They eventually settled in the Atlin district of British Columbia, where they ran a café at Spruce Creek for many years. Atlin was then and still is a resort to which many Juneau residents fly for their holidays.

Jack London wrote "The Unexpected" six years after the actual events, heightening the drama of the situation by moving the locale a hundred miles farther up the coast and limiting the participants to those in the cabin. He then adds to the drama by building on the fears of the Nelsons, an excellent example of what a great writer can do to maximize suspense. Compared with the lonely death of Chuck Harborson, his story portrays the ultimate extreme of cabin fever.

3: GOLD CREEK

Back in Juneau most of my time was spent interviewing members of the state legislature, but on my days off a small ribbon of a stream called Gold Creek, which cascaded through Juneau's north end, drew me like a magnet, and I often rambled up the trail to its headwaters. One summer weekend I decided to investigate the empty shells of mines and buildings up there, while at the same time trying my luck with a gold pan. That there were remnants of this precious metal still to be found in the area was undeniable. Stories prevailed of freebooters who surreptitiously roamed the mines at considerable risk to chip away at the high-grade portions of ore bodies that remained in the abandoned shafts.

Descending into a mineshaft in search of quartz gold was not my idea of fun, but panning a creek for placer gold was another matter. My equipment consisted of one rather large pan and an army trenching tool of the sort that converts from a shovel to a pick depending on the mood of the operator and the texture of the soil. Other than these implements and the usual food supplies and camping gear, I toted a small mountain tent. Even though the skies were promising, my chief priority was to avoid getting caught shelterless in one of southeast Alaska's deluges.

As far as personal protection was concerned, a handgun of any kind was out. During a stint in the army as a military policeman I had found that even a barn door was safe from my aim. I also dismissed the idea of toting a rifle because it was too awkward to lug around. My complete lack of a protective arsenal, however, tended to affect my sense of security, the reason for this being the presence of the formidable Alaska brown bear, the largest species of grizzly in the world, which reserves the right to chase invaders out of his domain at his own convenience. So, with this in mind I brought along my bear-scarers—metal tent pegs tied to my pack so they clanked together every time I took a step. Of course, the problem with this defence mechanism was that it would also frighten away less menacing creatures such as deer or mountain goats.

I shouldered my pack at about six on a bright summery morning and climbed the grade on the east side of Juneau, passing the historic jail. Here an acquaintance of mine had once discovered an old batch of letters referring to the famous western gun fighter Wyatt Earp, advising the Alaska Territorial Police to confiscate his guns when he reached Juneau during the gold rush. One of these guns is exhibited in Juneau's Red Dog Saloon.

Farther up the hill I stopped to enjoy a magnificent view of Gastineau Channel, along which the burgeoning city of Juneau was clustered, and I tried to visualize what Juneau's harbour would have looked like in the days of Jack London, the narrator for the Klondike gold rush, and of George Carmack, the man who started it all. Continuing up the road past the city's reservoir, I trudged around a sharp curve and into Gold Creek Canyon. The road terminated here at the Alaska–Juneau Mine boarding house, which had been converted to a summer theatre and now featured a comedy entitled *Hootchinoo 'n Hotcakes*. This word *hootchinoo* had derived from the Tlingits' talents for taking a white man's product and improving on it. Whites had introduced rum to the local Natives, never suspecting they would not only learn how to concoct their own brand of spirits but turn around and market it back to the whites. In time the Tlingits became so good at making their own bootleg liquor that, when Chief Shakes and his brewmasters at their village of Wrangell refused a government order to destroy his stills, they were bombarded by the United States Navy. Now that over a hundred years have rubbed the veneer off the story, I would suspect that the bombardment resulted from plain ordinary jealousy: Shakes and his boys were making better booze than the white man. But their *hootchinoo* is remembered in the word "hooch," which became a synonym for illegal alcohol and was absorbed into the English language as well as into many others throughout the world.

Jack London did not ignore hooch in his writings. In fact, in his short story "A Hyperborean Brew" he demonstrates enough knowledge of the distilling process to impress even the most stoic of tipplers.

At that early hour on a summer morning the boarding house-cum-theatre was quiet, and I followed a fork in the road that took me to the left, not quite as far as the boarding house, and then crossed Gold Creek via a bridge. From here the road headed up the north side of the stream and soon disintegrated into a trail. The perpendicular slope of Mount Juneau was so close against the trail I could almost lean on it as I followed the narrowing path across Snow Slide Gulch, nervously peering down the 200-foot cliff on my right. The gulch was aptly named: two men who were surveying there earlier that year had narrowly missed being taken away by a slide.

The angle of the path lessened after crossing the gulch and

became more level thirty or forty feet above Gold Creek, and when the trail finally broke out of the canyon into a broader valley, I came upon a marker that read Granite Creek. I ascended a steep path for a short distance before it levelled off, and here I discovered that a trail crew had built a fireplace of loose rocks in a copse of isolated hemlocks. Deciding this would be a fine spot to enjoy my lunch, I sat down, took a sandwich out of my pack, and leaned back against a sturdy log. I had scarcely begun munching on my sandwich when a movement of some sort caught my eye, and after about two minutes out popped a little bewhiskered face at the base of a small footbridge some ten feet away. It was a weasel, his face reminding me of photos of "Soapy" Smith, the confidence man who had ramrodded the community of Skagway before he was killed in the summer of 1898. Soapy the weasel looked me over insolently and then disappeared, but as I proceeded to work on my ham sandwich, he again made an appearance, standing quietly with one paw raised, his head cocked to the side like a dog pointing a game bird at a field trial. I could see that he was sizing up the situation much as Smith did with marks at his gambling tables. The weasel then retreated into an intricate network of roots at the base of a hemlock, and I got up to check all the exits. Having no luck, I went back to my lunch in time to see the crafty little bandit make off with a piece of the ham. "All right, wise guy," I said softly, "you win." I left him another morsel of meat but imagined he would not bother with it because for him, like his namesake, the fun was in outwitting his victim.

The trail twisted through a gap from which Granite Creek bursts forth on the way to its junction with the Gold. The sight of the clear, bubbling water awakened such a thirst in me that it all but eliminated any inborn sense of precaution and I almost fell into the creek in my haste to get a drink. I drank deeply. Water in the north is the true nectar of the gods to a perspiring hiker. Its glacial sweetness is unique in the world.

The path edged upwards from this point, gradually angling away from the creek until several hundred feet of elevation separated the two. Here a section of the path about four feet in length had detached itself from the mountainside, leaving a treacherous gap. However, I inched around it with little trouble and continued upward and across a patch of snow before descending into Granite Creek basin, where I sat down to enjoy the magnificent vista before me. Jagged spires loomed to the east, part of the ridge lying between the waters of the Taku River and Gastineau Channel. The basin itself was partially filled by a small pond, which rested in a luxuriant shamrock-green meadow.

Since the day was well advanced, I put up my tent and made camp for the night, trusting to luck with respect to the ever-present grizzlies in the area and consoling myself with the thought that things could be worse. In times past there had been warlike aboriginals around to compound the danger, aboriginals who may have been responsible for the demise of the legendary first prospectors who ventured into Gold Creek, possibly by way of the same basin I was now in.

The adventures of these first gold seekers go hand in hand with the legend of the Lost Rocker Mine. Few mineralized areas in North America are without a Lost Rocker tale, but this one is better documented than most. During the summer of 1867, the year of the United States' purchase of Alaska, a prospector named Fred Culver was found more dead than alive adrift in a boat near the mile-wide mouth of the Taku River. (The peninsula on which the city of Juneau was eventually established is squeezed between this river and Gastineau Channel.) Captain Herbert G. Lewis of the Hudson's Bay Company ship *Otter* spotted the derelict boat off Stockade Point and ordered the man carried aboard. That Culver possessed a poke of gold estimated to be worth $1,800 did not go unnoticed by the captain or his crew, but when Culver was asked where he found the gold, he was vague. He told the captain that he and his two companions had beached their canoe on the west side of the Taku River and from that point had followed a stream as far as possible uphill then crossed a ridge to the headwaters of another creek, the source of which was a small pond. They descended the creek until it flowed into another rivulet, and it was in this stream bed that they found coarse gold. They built a rocker box (which is more efficient than a gold pan) and worked the creek for two weeks before they were attacked by Natives. The prospector said his two companions were killed immediately but he grabbed one of the bags of gold and ran for his life, scrambling back the way he had come. He managed to reach the boat they had hidden on the shore and shoved off into the Taku River, barely escaping his pursuers, who could not follow because they did not have boats.

This last fact tends to make the story sound implausible because, like the Natives of the plains and their horses, Alaska coastal Natives are seldom without their canoes. Thus, circumstanccs would have had to be considerably out of the ordinary for a white man to escape by water from a coastal tribe bent on his destruction. However, if Culver's attackers were Auks, a people who reside on the other side of the mountains from the Taku River, it would explain why they would not have their canoes with them to continue the chase after he reached his boat.

From where I was camped, I could well visualize the incident because the geography matched Culver's memory of it. The little pond was immediately in front of me and from it dribbled the brook that forms Granite Creek, which then tumbles into Gold Creek. The headlands above the basin are steep but not inaccessible, and a man could make it across them, particularly if he was spurred on by knowledge that his life depended on it!

I had wondered how Culver evaded the surprise attack in the first place, but taking the flora of the country into consideration, I could more readily understand. My camp was at the upper end of the foliage line, and immediately below it were bush berries, devil's club, alder and the myriad forms of buck brush that are almost impossible to walk through. My guess was that, when the Auks realized Culver had escaped, they looked for him downstream, not upstream, and by the time it dawned on them that the prospectors had come over the mountains from the east, Culver had been far enough ahead of them to bolt over the crest of the mountains to safety.

Numerous expeditions were subsequently launched to find the site of the gold discovery, but its location remained lost to everyone, including Culver. It seems likely, however, that the creek he described was the same one on which Dick Harris and Joe Juneau found gold thirteen years later, and that being the case, the Lost Rocker Mine had not really been lost, only misplaced for a while. Of course, if their discovery was not the same one as Culver's, it means there is a bona fide gold-bearing creek out there somewhere waiting to be rediscovered.

Descending Granite Creek the next morning, just as Culver may have done in 1867, my hike took me back to Gold Creek. This time my direction was to the left, up through the mists hanging over the stream until Silver Bow Basin hove into view. As the headwaters of Gold Creek, this had been the site of much of the mining activity in the area, and there were enough prospect holes, shafts, tunnels and stopes to accommodate a community of prairie dogs. Picking my way among the remnants of what had once been a thriving mining camp, I thought of Juneau and Harris. Their quest for gold had been underwritten by an investor—otherwise known as a "grubstaker"—by the name of George Pilz, a mining engineer who had tried unsuccessfully to open a gold property near Sitka, then capital of the newly purchased Alaska Territory. When this venture failed, Pilz raised more funds to prospect likely areas in southeastern Alaska, locating them in a unique manner: he sent word out to the various Native bands that he would give them one hundred blankets in return for samples of minerals. Some worthy samples were delivered by Kowee, chief of the Auks who were then residents of Auke Bay, and one of these would later be called Gold Creek.

To follow up these leads, Pilz hired twelve men, two of them being Dick Harris and Joe Juneau. As a consequence, the two prospectors found themselves paddling up Gastineau Channel in the summer of 1880 where they met the geologist John Muir and missionary Samuel Hall Young. In 1915, some thirty-five years after the fact, Young recorded this meeting in his book, *Alaska Days with John Muir.* He and Muir had camped one night on a creek, then nameless, which he later decided must have been Gold. The next day they set out by boat to catch a tide high enough to get them through Gastineau Channel to Stevens Passage. On the way they met Harris and Juneau, and the two boats rendezvoused long enough to chat about their respective destinations. The two gold seekers then asked Muir and Young where they had camped, and when Muir told them, Harris turned to his partner and suggested they camp at the same creek and pan its gravel. Then they paddled off to their date with destiny.

Whether Muir actually told them that gold could be found along the creek is unclear in Young's book, nor is there any reference to it in Muir's writings. However, it seems likely that Muir, with his expertise as a geologist, would have offered that information. Young gave the two prospectors the credit they richly deserved for the discovery, though some kudos are doubtlessly in order for Chief Kowee and George Pilz as well. However, when I met Dick Harris's grandson of the same name, a lanky, light-haired, blue-eyed man whose forebears were both white and First Nations, he had a gripe about the treatment his grandfather had received. At first, everything had gone well between the partners, but after a few years a legal hassle had ensued, forcing Grandpa Harris to forfeit his claims at a considerable loss, and he never really recovered from this setback. He died twenty years later in Portland, Oregon, in a home sponsored by the Masonic Order, of which he was a member. But the crowning blow to his fortunes came when the name of the 160-acre townsite the two prospectors had staked and christened Harrisburg was changed to Juneau because postal authorities figured it would be confused with Pennsylvania's capital city.

My snooping brought me to the foot of a ridge at the head of Gold Creek valley, upon which a rickety, weathered structure stood, towering over the landscape and invoking for me the image of a Buddhist temple in far-off Tibet—or a haunted house. But this huge frame building had once been the Perseverance Mine's boarding house, constructed in 1887 by George Pilz, the man responsible for the search by Harris and Juneau. He had also built a mill here, only to lose it when California financiers withdrew their backing for the project. Later, the Perseverance was taken over by the Alaska–Juneau Company, which undercut the mountain above the boarding house to create a huge glory hole a quarter of a mile across.

The mist had burned away by this time and the nearby peaks, which had looked ruggedly indifferent when enveloped by clouds, now turned yellow in the sun. This put me in an optimistic frame of mind for gold panning, a simple process by which gravel is put into a gold pan, water added and the pan rocked around until all the gravel has been washed away, leaving the gold. But panning is also an art and a test of patience, strength, and willpower. It takes strength of the legs to be able to squat for hours while swirling cold water in a pan, and it takes a strong will to keep both hands holding onto the gold pan while the ever-present mosquitoes enjoy a lengthy lunch at the panner's expense.

As I panned, I thought of the traditional wandering prospectors about whom Jack London wrote, "They forgot the world and its ways as the world had forgotten them; killed their meat as they found it; feasted in plenty and starved in famine, and searched unceasingly for the yellow lure." Though most are gone now, there are still a few individuals around who come close to that old image. They are usually pretty good woodsmen, accepting as a matter of course what a mountain climber might consider a real adventure. They live off the land or get by on sparse rations for weeks at a time. This independence carries over into their equipment; if they must travel "light" to a particularly inaccessible place, they even disdain sleeping gear, opting to keep warm by lying against a log they have set afire on the underside. They have no ambition other than to satisfy their immediate needs and to pursue their own quest for an elusive strike. They are usually more compatible with nature than they are with the ersatz complexities of human association. They do not believe in progress in the traditional sense; to them progress means living at peace with their fellow man by not living with him at all.

As I squatted with my hands in freezing water only minutes out of a glacier, my thoughts also drifted to the so-called benefits of progress whether it is in Alaska or anywhere else. Where were we all going? If smog, freeways, and traffic jams were examples of progress, maybe a little retrogression was in order. Possibly, I decided, the prospector has found what most of us have spent a lifetime looking for. Maybe we need a good, backward-looking leader to take us in his direction.

After a few hours I reluctantly concluded that my panning project on Upper Gold Creek was a lost cause as my predecessors had swept it clean. I quit the creek, and a walk of only a few yards brought me to the foot of the ridge upon which the Perseverance boarding house presided. Hoisting my pack onto my back, I commenced to climb. This pack was an enlarged army version of the famous Norwegian Bergan pack, which was really designed for skiing as it hangs low in the back with the weight resting on the hips. It is therefore preferable to the standard pack board when travelling in the thick bush of southeast Alaska because the tips of the standard board stick out above one's head and frequently catch on low alder or willow branches. For the hiker using an aluminum pack board this can be exasperating as he cannot saw the tips off.

My low-slung pack did not hinder me on my scramble through the thick brush toward the boarding house, but halfway up the rise one foot slipped, leaving me with the unenviable choice of falling down the incline or grasping the stem of a devil's club plant to prevent it. I opted for the devil's club. The next time I'll take the fall. That stroke of misguided brilliance resulted in my hand looking like a pincushion, swollen and burning. Devil's club is an enigma of nature's scheme of things: it has the leaves of a maple tree, the trunk of a palm tree, and the needles of a cactus, and this insidious plant not only sports spines on its stalk but also on the undersides of its foliage. One thing this accident did do for me was provide entertainment for the night that followed—digging the spines out of my hand. There is a knack to this learned long ago by old-timers: you wait until the tiny wounds fester, then you pop out the needles. I consoled myself that my problem could have been worse; I've heard stories of cheechakos (the Native Alaskan term for "newfie") using devil's club leaves for toilet paper!

Having avoided a fall and regained my composure, I made another effort and reached the top of the rise and thus gained access to the boarding house, a monstrous structure in a glorious setting. Although it was rickety, the roof was firm, and as twilight came on the stairs led me to the top floor where I unrolled my sleeping bag in one of the small rooms at the end of the east wing. Inscriptions on the wall dated back thirty long years to when the nearby Alaska–Juneau Mine was in operation. Finn Gronvold wrote: "June 5, 1937. Be coming back sometime." I wondered if he ever made it. Another man simply inscribed the times of his arrival and departure: "Walt Blaskowsky, Olympia, Washington, April 21, 1941. Arrived Juneau July 9, 1940. Leaving June 10, 1941." These inscriptions set loose a flood of nostalgia. What was it like here when the boarding house was alive with activity? What had inspired these men to come, and where were they now—if they were still alive?

I found myself musing over the coincidence that brought me into contact with this last relic of the Alaska–Juneau Mine after having bought and sold its stocks only a few years earlier when I was working on the floor of the New York Stock Exchange. The mine itself had been closed during World War II, and now its hallowed shafts were only frequented by the occasional high-grader. When I had interviewed one of them and asked what it was like to partake in such illegal activity, his answer had been characteristically blunt: "If you could miniaturize yourself and descend into an abandoned beehive in the dark, you would get a pretty good idea." The first problem, he said, was to find your way into the mine. This was not easy because the company hired watchmen to keep people out, but since the complex was so extensive it was all but impossible for them to watch every passage. "Once inside, you head for a place you think will be a profitable spot to pan tailings or to knock off a choice chunk of high grade ore." He said he had been looking for the "jewel room," the room where extra high-grade ore was added to average-yield material to increase the gold or silver assay, but as yet had not found it.

To look for gold, he said, "You should have a flashlight with you as well as a couple of candles. If you plan to stay in there for any length of time, you want to bring a sleeping bag and food. You must exercise some caution. If, for example, you lose your flashlight, there is always the possibility of stumbling over ancient boxes of dynamite caps and primers. And when that stuff has been sitting there for twenty years, even thinking about them can set the caps off." He summed up his "occupation" by saying it was more exciting than it was profitable. I had the distinct impression that if Alaska–Juneau had given him permission to high-grade, he would not have bothered!

Sleep was all but impossible that night in the old boarding house. There were just too many spectres clanking around—not with chains but with picks and shovels. In one of those intervals Jack London entered my thoughts. His roving eyes had not missed the significance of Silver Bow Basin, and he mentions it briefly in his "Gold Hunters of the North," but as far as I could discern it never entered his fiction.

A decade after I spent my night in the Perseverance boarding house, it burned to the ground. I'm told that only a few charred timbers now mark the spot.

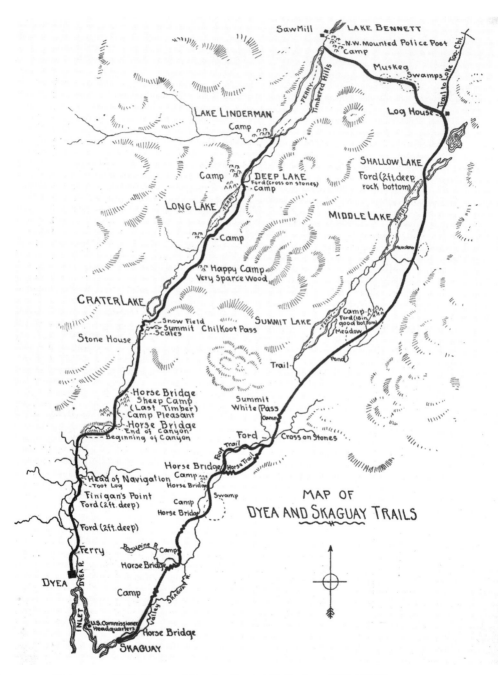

University of Washington Libraries, Special Collections, UW 16622

4: A KLONDIKE GATEWAY

Achance to follow the gold rush route came in September 1964. The heads of the governments of Alaska, British Columbia, and the Yukon Territory had scheduled a meeting for Whitehorse in the middle of the month. When I sought out the editor of the *Empire*, Darwin Lambert, and requested the chance to cover it, he said okay and gave me two weeks vacation as well. Travelling to the Yukon capital would give me a good chance to assess Jack London's perambulations, and with luck a canoe trip down the Yukon River might even be arranged. The very next day I boarded the Alaska mainline ferry the MV *Malaspina* for the journey up Lynn Canal to Skagway.

In his essay "Gold Hunters of the North," London traces the adventures of some of the men whose curiosity took them across the Chilkoot Pass to look for gold. "Like hound dogs," he writes, "they followed the scent of gold up the coast into the interior, scaling insurmountable passes and forbidding glaciers, battling torrential creeks, until one day they reached the Klondike, and the boom was on."

One of the earliest of these "hound dogs" was George

Carmack. He set up a tent camp in Juneau and eventually persuaded a party of adventurers to join him in searching for gold across the coast range in the Yukon River valley. Later, he made the ultimate discovery—the pot at the end of the subarctic rainbow—when he and two Native men struck it rich at Rabbit (renamed Bonanza) Creek in what was then the Northwest Territories of Canada. The date was August 17, 1896.

News of the extent of the strike reached "outside" ports when the first ships laden with gold returned south the following summer. San Francisco virtually exploded with excitement, and when twenty-one-year-old Jack London heard about it, he scurried around Oakland trying to rustle up funds to join the rush. Previous loans from friends, including his pal John Heinold, had narrowed his options. Finally, he pedalled his bike up a long hill in east Oakland, hoping he could hire on to assist the famous journalist and poet Joaquin Miller, who had been commissioned by the *San Francisco Examiner* to cover the gold rush. When he discovered that Miller had already left for the Klondike he turned instead to his stepsister Eliza London and her husband J.H. "Cap" Shepard, painting such a vivid picture of the incentives of a Klondike venture that his sixty-year-old brother-in-law was bitten by the fever. In the end Shepard refused to advance the funds unless London took him along. Sandbagged, he acquiesced. The Shepards mortgaged their house to pay for the journey.

Paying thirty dollars each for their tickets, London and Shepard set out from San Francisco aboard the *Umatilla* on July 23, 1897. (On the passenger list published in the *San Francisco Examiner*, London's name was misspelled as Gondon.) Also aboard were three men from Santa Rosa whom London and his brother-in-law would befriend and link up with as partners. These three had several other things in common. They were all older than London, two of them by at least twenty years. They were successful at what they did. And they were non-drinkers—unlike London!

Fred Thompson was a tall, square-jawed, clean shaven, garrulous Santa Rosa court reporter in his forties. In keeping with his profession, he studiously maintained a diary throughout the Klondike trip. Jim Goodman was also a big man and about the same age as Thompson. Dark-eyed, he sported a close-cropped beard and moustache. He and his brother Dan ran a small farm and ranch in the Mark West area of Santa Rosa. J. Merritt Sloper was a pal of Jim's brother Dan. An excellent carpenter and boat builder, he was only slightly older than London, and shorter than London's five feet seven inches.

An enthusiastic crowd was on hand to see the *Umatilla* sail, and next day the *Examiner* reported:

> On to the Klondyke! That was the cry of the three-score fortune-seekers who sailed on the Pacific Coast steamship *Umatilla* yesterday morning. The cry was taken up by the thousands assembled on the dock to bid farewell to the adventurous band until it was heard for blocks.

The steamer was scheduled to leave around 9 a.m. but was an hour and a half late because of the huge quantity of supplies brought down at the last minute by Yukon-bound travellers. In fact, several tons of beans and canned goods were left on the dock for lack of space in the ship's hold. As it was, the steamer was loaded so haphazardly that it listed considerably to port before the problem was resolved.

The trip to Port Townsend, Washington, was generally uneventful except for some rough weather, which caused most of London's fellow passengers to get seasick. Having been before the mast and having piloted his own boat around San Francisco Bay for many years, he was immune to this malady. After a brief stop in Victoria, British Columbia, where London and Shepard purchased some supplies, the ship continued to Port Townsend. Here, London and his new partners unloaded their gear and spent the night in the city jail because no other facilities were available. The next day they boarded the *City of Topeka* for the rest of the voyage up the Inside Passage via Wrangell to Juneau.

According to Fred Thompson's journal, it poured rain from the time they arrived in Juneau until they left on August 5 for Dyea, eighty miles to the north. This port was the gateway to the Chilkoot Pass over which London and his partners would hike to reach the headwaters of the Yukon River.

Thompson's journal does not expand on their adventures in Juneau, nor does it mention where they stayed, but I have assumed that, like Carmack many years earlier, they lived in a

The *City of Topeka* carried London and Shepard from Port Townsend, Washington to Juneau, Alaska. *University of Washington Libraries, Special Collections, PH Coll 273*

tent. London's papers are equally vague about this, but perhaps he, Thompson, Cap Shepard, Goodman and Sloper were all too preoccupied transferring their material from the ship to the canoes of the Tlingits they had hired to transport them to Dyea.

The route of the *Malaspina* was the same as that followed by Jack London with one exception: London's group had paddled straight north from Juneau by way of the shallow Gastineau Channel, whereas the ferry was forced to go south into deep water and then swing around Douglas Island to head north again. Unlike my previous quick trips to Haines and Skagway in the depths of winter when the skies were overcast and visibility poor, this September day was clear and warm, bringing out the best nature had to offer. Porpoises played in the water while overhead eagles glided on the air currents, their piercing eyes searching for fish. Killer whales were in abundance, their giant dorsal fins announcing their presence.

But while I watched the passing scene, I was pondering one aspect of London's trip north that didn't add up for me. Why would he and his associates hire Native people to take them up Lynn Canal when it would have been much simpler and more comfortable aboard a ship? It was possible that they simply could not afford passage, of course, though a more likely explanation may be that they had heard ghastly stories of stampeders' goods being dumped onto the tidal flats when the tide was out, only to be engulfed by the sea when the tide came in. Using canoes, they could float in with the tide right up to the high water mark. Or it may have been faster to paddle north: what with boat schedules, loading and unloading, they may have figured they could beat a steamship. It also may have been that the *City of Topeka* on which they arrived in Juneau did not go farther north. Whatever the reason for their choice, Thompson did record that they ran their canoes ashore at Dyea at 3:30 p.m. on August 5, 1897.

My own journey along Lynn Canal was luxurious compared to London huddled over the thwarts of his canoe. From the comfort of a deck chair, I studied the mountains to the east reaching skyward, their emerald glaciers dripping like huge frozen tears off the ponderous Juneau icefield. The snow smothering the ice looked like a bulky white comforter. On the west side of the Canal the radiant, snow-embossed peaks of the Chilkat range faded into the horizon in the direction of Haines. We passed Horse Island, Bernier's Bay and the infamous Eldred Rock, a partially submerged protuberance now guarded by a lighthouse. Unmarked in London's day, it had punctured many a ship's hull.

Ultimately we glided past Haines, Alaska, off our port side, and I thought back to a quick trip I had made there the previous winter with Chuck Keen, an ex-logger turned cinematographer. He had landed a contract to film the first winter opening of the Haines Road, an artery connecting the newly instituted Marine Highway system with the Alaska Highway at Haines Junction in Canada and, farther up the line, tying the arm of southeast Alaska into the mainland mass of the state. Keen and I had briefly visited the Totem Bowl, a bar and bowling alley in Port Chilkoot, a suburb of Haines, which had once been an army fort. We met the bartender, Wesley Willard, whose Chilkat grandfather had adopted his surname from Eugene Willard, the first white man to establish a mission in the area. Willard filled us in on the local history.

"Reverend Samuel Hall Young and John Muir came here in a canoe guided by some Tlingits around 1875," he said. "Young noticed there were a lot of Native people around here and figured it would be a good place for a mission. He told Reverend Willard to follow up on it, and that's how we got the mission. It was called Haines Station at that time."

The original station was built at the foot of a number of trails leading inland from the coast, and Willard's timing in establishing it was more than satisfactory from the standpoint of missionary work. By briefing the Natives on the idiosyncrasies of the white race, he and his wife alleviated some of the cultural shock when Caucasians overran them less than two decades later.

"Where'd the name Haines come from?" I asked, at the same time eyeing a swing that hung over the saloon's dance floor.

"It was named for a lady [Mrs. E.F. Haines] who had made a big donation to the Presbyterian Church," Willard said.

"What's the swing for?" I asked.

"Swinging!" he replied with a laugh. "See those marks on the ceiling? If you got the guts or enough drinks, you can hit the roof with your feet."

Keen shook his head in disbelief. "Who pays for the insurance on the place?"

"I don't know, but we haven't had any injuries or lawsuits yet," Willard replied.

Wes Willard was an interesting individual in his own right. He had only recently returned from the New York World's Fair where he had been commissioned to carve a huge totem pole. "I guess," he said as we left, "I'm the only bartender in the world who has a second job as a totem pole whittler."

Jack London, though he never visited Haines, knew about the area, and he acknowledged Eugene Willard's legacy in several of his short stories. In his "The Grit of Women," a man named Sitka Charley and his Chilkat mate, Passuk, head for the mission at Haines to seek relief for miners who are starving at the gold camp at Forty Mile. These messengers have mushed seven hundred miles up the Yukon River when, at Caribou Crossing, the Chilkat woman dies in the arms of her companion. Spurred on by the memory of her unselfish love, Sitka Charley plods across the snow and ice and sub-zero temperatures of the Chilkoot Pass to reach the mission.

In real life Sitka Charley was one of the guides for John Muir and Samuel Hall Young on their first trip to the Chilkat's domain in 1879. Of him Muir wrote, "Charley, the youngest of my crew, noticing my interest in glaciers, said that when he was a boy he had gone with his father to hunt seals in a large bay full of ice (Glacier Bay), and though it was long since he had been there, he thought he could find his way to it." London adopted Sitka Charley in a literary sense and spun several yarns around him. In "Siwash," he demonstrated his knowledge of the aboriginal ways as well as a passing familiarity with the geography and climate of the Lynn Canal coast, and near the end of the story he invoked the name of the Haines Mission as the place where the girl, Killisnoo, dies. Wrote London, "And then she died, in the heart of the winter, died in childbirth, up there on the Chilkat Station. She held my hand to the last, the ice creeping up inside the door and spreading thick on the gut of the window."

Ultimately, W.H. Dall, a renowned expert on Native culture, criticized London for his unrealistic portrayals of the Natives of the extreme northwest. While this may be true to an extent, London certainly mastered the psychology of the aboriginal mind in his writing. An excellent example is provided in "Siwash" where the protagonist understands the pride and superstitions of the indigenous people and capitalizes on them to kidnap a woman slated to marry a chief of the Tlingits. So while the plot may be far-fetched, it is a good yarn.

As is often the case in North America, the Native people of this area had already established most of the paths that would become roads after the whites arrived. The present Haines Road follows the route used by the Tlingits when they climbed over the coastal range to descend into the valleys of the upper Yukon basin in order to trade with the Sticks who lived inland. Their purpose was to swap such products as eulachon oil for items they needed. Trade with the Sticks complemented that with the

Chilkats, a sub-tribe of the Tlingits, by supplying them with moose hides, moccasins decorated with porcupine quills, birch bows wound with porcupine gut, copper pounded into sheets, and caribou hides along with the sinews and *babiche* made from them. In return, the Chilkats supplied the Sticks with shell ornaments and cedar bark baskets.

The scene changed with the arrival of white traders along the coast. Their seemingly insatiable demand for furs played right into the hands of the shrewd coastal tribes, and the latter began reaping huge profits as middle men between the whites and the Sticks, who accessed the highest grade of furs. Now the Tlingits began carrying powder and shot, guns, woollen blankets, beads, iron kettles, knives, axes and assorted wearing apparel across the mountains, exchanging them for the furs of fox, beaver, otter, wolf and wolverine. And it was this trade that indirectly gave rise to the entire gold rush. As early as 1848, the Chilkats had carried "paper that talks" between a Captain Dodd of the Hudson's Bay ship *Beaver* and Robert Campbell, who was building the Bay's trading post, Fort Selkirk, at the confluence of the Pelly and the Yukon rivers. This was some three hundred miles inland from Klukwan, the largest Tlingit village on the coastal side of the mountains. Chief Kohklux and his men were not able to read the letters they carried back and forth but could well guess their significance. Plainly, if the white men succeeded in building a trading post in the interior, they would make serious inroads into the monopoly Kohklux's people held in their trade with the Sticks. But the chief was patient. Four years went by before he launched an expedition against Fort Selkirk, drove the invaders away and destroyed the post, effectively expelling the whites from the interior and preserving the Tlingits' trade routes for another twenty years.

The Chilkat Trail, which during the gold rush of 1896–98 followed the old Tlingit route, may have been only a sideshow to the main event that was taking place on the Chilkoot Pass, but it had an important role to play in that story. Its principal publicist was Jack Dalton, one of the first explorers to cross the coastal mountains via this route. Dalton paid the Tlingits for the right to improve on the trail then charged a toll for the gold seekers who used it.

Once Haines was behind us, the *Malaspina* passed the little fjord on our starboard side where London and his group had turned off on their way to Dyea. We could see the distant peaks that hovered over their route, a formidable horde, indeed. During the gold rush the Dyea people had actively competed with Skagway for the business of the stampeders, describing their route as "steeper but quicker." Later they had even built a tramline to expedite the hauls, though that was after London and his friends had passed through. According to Fred Thompson's journal, the group's first day ashore at Dyea was spent assembling their supplies in one spot while at the same time making sure they were above the highest reaches of the tidal bore, which here varies by more than twenty feet. They were not alone on the beach because a whole load of Argonauts had been dumped there by the steamship *Elder* that same day. And they knew that hundreds more steamers were plying steadily northward to deposit their human cargo at Dyea and at Skagway, each one regurgitating its share of stampeders bent on participating in what would be for most a vain, flamboyant folly.

After assembling all their supplies, London and his partners rested on their second day there, August 8, 1897. Facing them were the precipitous peaks of the coast range, which loomed over the shore like an impenetrable wall, the only crack in this bastion being the notch called Chilkoot Pass. The trail to it climbed 3,600 feet in just sixteen miles, with the last 500 feet almost straight up. Once they reached the summit, it would be downhill another sixteen miles to Lake Bennett, where they would have to build a boat and launch it for the passage through the upper lakes in order to reach the Yukon River seventy-six miles beyond Bennett.

When someone explained to the partners that by towing a boat with their goods aboard up the Taiya River they could avoid six miles of backpacking as well as a sharp hill at the very beginning of the trail, London wandered around the beach until he found a boat and purchased it for ten dollars. Thompson's diary notes that on August 9 they began the process of loading it up with all the supplies it would hold then using a tow line to haul it five miles up the river to a point called "the head of navigation." It took them three days to complete these relays.

Next they headed up the trail, each man toting what his strength would allow. The task of carrying supplies up to the Pass was compounded by regulations set forth by the Northwest Mounted Police, which required all gold-seekers entering Canada to have at least a thousand pounds of food with them. But since the stampeders also needed to bring additional clothing, tools, bedding, a stove and shelter, the total load per person could reach 1,500 to 2,000 pounds. The advantages of partnerships were, therefore, quite obvious—four partners, for example, needed only one stove, one boat and one tent and the work of carrying them was divided four ways. The Mounties also required each stampeder to have five hundred dollars in cash, though they were more lax about this than about food. Plainly, they did not want to have a bunch of starving would-be miners on their hands once freeze-up shut down all contact with the outside world.

London was very much aware of the problems involved in toting supplies. In his book *Smoke Bellew* he calculated that a man carrying a little less than one hundred pounds per load while relaying a total of eight hundred pounds for two miles actually walked thirty-eight miles. Pro-rating this figure for the entire thirty-mile trail meant the distance walked would be over five hundred miles, and more than half of this distance was uphill! And for London the job was doubled because he was not only packing his own supplies but also those of his brother-in-law, who at sixty was suffering terribly from rheumatism. Realization of the

magnitude of the group's task began to set in at the end of their first day of backpacking. They had made so little progress that they had to alter their plans, and the following day, August 13, they sent three thousand pounds of supplies by Native packers to the top of the Pass. For this service they were charged $660.

The amount of money spent on packing services is one of the fascinating aspects of the gold rush. At least three hundred men were pouring into the Chilkoot Pass funnel on any given day, and since it took each of them at least a month to travel the roughly thirty miles of the trail and each man had about a ton of supplies, at any given time there were nine thousand men on trail packing a total of eighteen million pounds of provisions. And since probably a third of this weight was packed across the Pass at the going rate of twenty cents a pound,

Gold-seekers (and gold rush photographers like Frank LaRoche, shown pushing the barge) were required to haul at least a thousand pounds of food, plus clothing, tools, bedding, a stove and shelter. *University of Washington Libraries, Special Collections, LaRoche 2011*

professional packers were taking in roughly $1.3 million a month.

In 1963, a year before my trip on the *Malaspina*, I had visited the Dyea "harbour" with Chuck Keen and Skagway's giant police chief Bert Finlay. We had driven eight miles around the point west of Skagway and descended a long hill overlooking the beach. The silence was so overwhelming that even the squawk of a raven would have been welcome. Every vestige of what had once been a thriving port was gone so that it was hard to imagine what it had been like. And it must have been something to see— a sort of World War II invasion without the gunfire—jammed with gold rushers, horses, dogs, crates, furniture and mountains of canned foods, all of them dumped unceremoniously on the tidal flats. As often as not, the supplies were within reach of Lynn Canal's salty tentacles and had to be moved quickly to avoid ruin. Plainly and simply, it must have been a mess.

Bert Finlay took us to meet the "Mayor of Dyea," Emil Hanousek, who'd had no trouble getting elected as he was the only resident. He was not an untypical relic of the back country in that his cabin was spotless. His cot could have passed an army inspection, and each cup, plate, fork, knife and spoon had its special station.

We discussed the progress of the restoration of the Chilkoot Pass trail on which Hanousek had been working. After the frantic surge for gold was over, forest growth had closed in on the millions of forgotten steps, leaving nothing but memories and sporadic traces of a path. The restoration project was under the supervision of the Youth and Adult Authority of the State of Alaska but directed by Mike Leach of the Alaska Forest Service. The job included building cabins at Canyon City and Sheep Camp on the Chilkoot Pass trail as well as clearing the path itself. According to Hanousek, it was one tough job.

He also told us of a couple, Barb and Ed Kalen, who were the last two people to hike the Pass before World War II. "Once they had ventured through the willows and buck brush for about ten miles," said Hanousek, "they realized it would be easier to go on than to turn back, and when they finally came out on the railroad at Bennett, their clothes were virtually in rags.

"The problem we have now," he continued, "are the hikers who are going in before we finish. The Canadian side is not being worked on, so the result is lost hikers. With the money we expend fishing 'em out of there with helicopters, we could rebuild the trail three times over."

Three years after our talk with Hanousek, the *Yukon Daily News* campaigned to clear the trail on the Canadian side by helping Dick Morrow, chief of the Yukon's Department of Corrections, to obtain permission from British Columbia to do the work. It gives me great satisfaction to have played a role in that successful endeavour.

Disembarking from the *Malaspina* at Skagway on this late summer day in 1964, I was more favourably impressed by the little community than I had been on that previous mid-winter visit. Directly north, the Skagway River plummeted down through a series of gorges to nourish the triangular valley where the town stood amid an exuberant growth of conifers. A lush population of cultivated flowers and berries also abounded because Skagway reaps the benefits of the Pacific Ocean's summer winds, and many of the local inhabitants were prolific gardeners. But summers here are in sharp contrast to the raging blasts of cold that rip the town in winter when masses of Arctic air pour out of the interior and down White Pass to fasten Skagway in an icy grip. In fact, it was this wind that gave Skagway its name. Derived from the Tlingit word *Skoogwa*, it refers to an old woman who, legend says, was the valley's saviour as she kept it free of snow simply by blowing it away. The only trouble with *Skoogwa* was that her lungs were filled with cold air rather than warm. But I know many residents would happily welcome the snow in exchange for a blast of hot air in the depths of winter.

Rumours persist to this day that Jack London drifted over to Skagway from Dyea and invaded the Pack Train Bar on his way north. According to Fred Thompson's diary he did not, though the real-life dog hero of London's book *The Call of the Wild* did visit the Pack Train with his masters, the brothers Louis and Marshall Bond, and their friend Stanley Pearce, an English mining engineer. The Bonds had left Seattle several weeks before London departed from San Francisco. Prior to embarking, Louis Bond purchased two dogs: a full-bred St. Bernard named "Pat" and a St. Bernard–German shepherd cross called "Jack"—later immortalized by London as "Buck." Marshall Bond's son, in his book about his father, *Gold Hunter*, describes the Pack Train Bar as nothing but a huge tent with log walls. When the three men went inside, it is reasonable to assume the dogs came in with them as they were too valuable to leave unattended.

Quickly finding the Pack Train, which by good luck was open, I sought out the popular proprietor Magee Brenna, who was doling out drinks. The very aura of the place crackled with the vibes of history, and cornering Brenna, I asked him flat out if London or Buck had ever been in there.

Magee shook his derby-crowned head and said, "You hear all sorts of talk. One rumour was that Buck was here, and another was that Jack was here, but that they were not here together."

That tied in with what I already knew. Imposters had plagued Jack London after he became famous. Once a Billings, Montana, bank dunned him for two bad cheques; he responded by sending them a copy of his signature and informing them he had never been in Billings in his life other than passing through on a train. A hobo wrote a book about travelling across North

America with him, 90 percent of it untrue. Another man impersonating London journeyed throughout Alaska in 1900–1902, and some people in Nome are still convinced that he was in that town during those years, though he never visited Nome in his life.

Bolting my beer, I thanked Magee and slipped outside to look the town over. The city was spread at the foot of Face Mountain—so named because its outline resembles a Native face in profile—with Harding Peak looming to the southwest. Skagway did not have much room to expand, but this did not seem to worry its inhabitants. Since its inception it has been a thriving seaport and a focal point for transshipping mineral wealth out of the Yukon Territory while bringing in supplies and equipment. The White Pass and Yukon Route Company was the hub of this activity with its railroad and ships holding a virtual monopoly, and though Skagway was an "open" town as opposed to a "company" one, most of its residents were company employees. There was, however, an economically viable minority consisting of fishermen, loggers, government representatives and lastly storekeepers and innkeepers catering to the tourist trade.

I could see that Skagway had not lost its flair for capitalizing on its influx of visitors. Travellers disembarking from ferries and steamships always began their visits by strolling along the lengthy wharf that took them from the present, as evidenced by their ship, to the past, as exemplified by the town itself. With its breathtaking scenery, false-fronted buildings, honky-tonk music, dirt roads, old saloons and rustic hotels, it was indeed an appealing place.

That night I stayed at the Skagway Inn, and the next morning when the whistle tooted to announce that the train was ready for the trip to Whitehorse, I hurriedly loaded my suitcase and pack and hopped aboard. The engine jerked and then the low rumble of the wheels on the rails indicated we were on our way.

Left to right: Marshall Bond, canine Jack, prototype for Buck of *The Call of the Wild*, Oliver Lafarge, Lyman Colt, Stanley Pearce, and Pat, the St. Bernard. *Marshall Bond, University of New Mexico Press*

The locomotive gradually built up momentum, but its speed was only a few miles an hour greater than that of a turtle as we commenced the climb to White Pass, a climb that would take us from sea level to 2,885 feet in only twenty miles. Thus we climbed from summer into fall.

As the train inched toward the notch, the vibrant splash of the foliage camouflaged the more sinister aspects of the Pass's history. Lower by eight hundred feet than neighbouring Chilkoot Pass, it was no less deadly in beckoning the unwary into its swampy mires during the gold rush. They were also confronted with disease, one of the most dangerous being spinal meningitis, which reached epidemic proportions in 1897–98, causing scores of men to die on the White Pass trail and causing many more to become permanently disabled. Other aspects of the route were just as ominous. An estimated five thousand men and one thousand horses fought their way through the forty-mile mud wallow called White Pass, and the toll on the horses was even more brutal than it was on the men. These poor beasts never had a chance as they had been weakened by undernourishment and overworked by men gripped with the madness for gold. Broken-down animals were expendable and in many cases were driven or pushed off the path to roll and tumble down into the maw of the canyon, which came to be known as Dead Horse Gulch. For the horses it was a one-way race to hell with no winner's circle.

Jack London, in his short story "Trust," which is about a man hiking through the pass, actually transferred the description of the White Pass sinkhole to the Chilkoot with which he was familiar. He wrote, "Part way down, the stars clouded over again, and in the consequent obscurity he slipped and rolled and slid for a hundred feet, landing bruised and bleeding on the bottom of a large shallow hole. From all about him arose the stench of dead horses. The hole was handy to the trail, and the packers had made a practice of tumbling into it their broken and dying animals. The stench overpowered him, making him death-ly sick, and as in a nightmare he scrambled out." It was only the construction of a narrow-gauge railway, initiated in 1898, that put an end to the ignominious practice of discarding worn-out horses by rolling them off the cliff.

The White Pass railway track had been laid out parallel to the trail for much of the distance to Lake Bennett, and as the train chugged along I noticed the flotsam of a bygone era still heaped along the right-of-way. But the most foreboding sight beside the tracks was Black Cross Rock, a deadly reminder of the beating that men and animals took while the railroad was under construction. At best, working conditions were dangerous with men perched like so many mountain goats amid the jagged cliffs, and accidents became so common that the workers began threatening to go on strike. This was the situation when one day a dynamite blast was signalled and workers scattered for sanctu-ary. Unfortunately, two of them sought refuge behind this huge rock and were killed when it was loosened by the blast and rolled over on top of them. After rumours flashed through the ranks of construction workers that sixteen men were under the boul-der, their leaders threatened a strike unless the railroad made some attempt to properly bury the men killed. Railroad engi-neers pointed out, however, that this would take a blast as strong as the one that moved the rock in the first place. Ultimately the company found out the names of the two men and marked the stone with a cross, and the strike was averted.

The view from the train was spectacular. At some points the drop-off into the valley was close to a thousand feet so that it felt more like being in an airplane than on a train. And no place depicted extreme changes in botanical zones better than this stretch of railroad from tidewater, where large conifers grew in abundance, to the crest of the Pass, where vegetation of any kind was almost non-existent. The exceptions were the tufts of purple scrub brush growing out of cracks in massive boulders strewn over the pre-Cambrian landscape and here and there the odd wind-whipped, contorted spruce clinging tenaciously to life by way of octopus-like roots that drained sustenance from the bleak ground. At the top of the Pass there was nothing for several miles but an eerie landscape of scattered potholes, then the route descended again into the forest to reach Lake Bennett. This general area on the other side of the Pass, including Lake Lindeman, was where the stampeders coming over the White and Chilkoot passes had converged to build the boats that would take them down the Yukon River to Dawson City.

Most of the stampeders chose the Chilkoot Pass over the White Pass because it was better organized. For example, the Healy and Wilson Trading Company ran a regularly scheduled twelve-horse pack train daily from the beach at Dyea to Sheep Camp, a distance of thirteen miles, and there was even a blacksmith's shop at Finnegan's Point. As well, many of the men on the Chilkoot route were veterans of the rushes for gold in California in 1849, Nevada's Comstock lode in the 1860s, and British Columbia's Caribou and Cassiar areas in the 1870s and '80s. However, these veterans were in almost unanimous agreement that there were more "tenderfeet" in the run for Klondike gold than they had seen before. There were literally scores of men who did not know how to shoe a horse or even throw a diamond hitch. Other men wore boots made of leather which froze solid at forty degrees below zero. Many came directly from life in the city and had little or no experience in cooking outdoors over an open fire, sleeping on the ground or putting up a wall tent.

Jack London and his companions were all experienced campers, and in addition each possessed a special skill that helped round out the partnership. Sloper was an expert at boat building, a talent that would be invaluable when they reached the headwaters of the Yukon River, and he also knew how to handle small

Dogsled team at Sheep Camp, Chilkoot Trail, Alaska, circa 1898. A sign in the background offers stampeders some of the comforts of home: "HOT drinks and meals, lunches and beds." *University of Washington Libraries, Special Collections, Hegg 85*

craft. Jim Goodman had prospected and logged in the western states and knew the difference between real gold and iron pyrite. A crack shot and experienced tracker, he would be the hunter for the group. Fred Thompson, a court reporter by trade, was clear of thought and orderly of character, and thus well suited to keeping a diary. Even on the worst days of the trip he managed to write a few lines in his journal, though being too busy to elaborate, he only recorded their party's progress in simple short sentences.

Fortunately, there were also two professional writers on the trail who were keeping notes as they travelled. The white-whiskered Joaquin Miller, hired by the *San Francisco Examiner* to cover the gold rush, was about three weeks ahead of London and his friends. Miller, at sixty-five, was a rugged character who had done everything from fighting Indians to publishing newspapers. Since his sponsor had underwritten the cost of packhorses, he had only his own pack to carry and could afford the time to look over the gold rush scene and write down his impressions. "Leaving Dyea," he observed, "we tramped along in line almost a mile, through the pleasantest of shady woods, summery, and sweet with flowers as high as my head on either hand. Pretty log cabins with Indians about the doors, old women knitting, girls drying fish, men mending nets and boats—a brighter scene, or more cheering, I do not hope to see…. A mile or so and I came to…piles and piles of primroses. A wild, swift river puts in here, a river sent rolling ahead, and plenty of birds and blossoms. A prettier walk than I found here on the bank of this swift river of birds and blossoms could not be found in the United States." Farther up the trail, he reported, "The water came tumbling down out of the clouds as at Yosemite, only here the great cataracts are too many to even count them much less name them. We have here truly a hundred Yosemites, a string of Yosemites for ten miles except that the walls of granite literally hang over us in places." As well, he noted patches of verdant grass as high as his shoulders and the best huckleberries he ever ate. He added that, like everything else in Alaska, they were the biggest in the world.

Tappan Adney, employed by *Harper's Weekly* to report on the gold rush, was about three weeks behind London. He started out from Dyea on August 31 and reached Finnegan's Point the same day. More pragmatic and businesslike than Miller, he reported on facts that would be of interest to those who were thinking of making the trip. For example, he wrote that at the tent hotel at Finnegan's Point, "a full meal of beans and bacon, bread and butter, dried peaches and coffee is served for six bits,

Joaquin Miller on the Chilkoot Pass trail. *University of Washington Libraries, Special Collections, LaRoche 10041 (cropped)*

or seventy-five cents." The worst part of the trail was in the canyon above the point, so he did not reach Sheep Camp until September 14. There he spent the night in the Palmer tent hotel sleeping on the floor under the dinner table. "When supper is over, the floor is thrown open for guests. All who have blankets unroll them and spread them on the floor, take off their socks and shoes and hang them on the rafters, place a coat under their heads and turn in."

Meanwhile, on August 14, as London and his party soldiered on, Cap Shepard called it quits. The day was very hot, and as he was now suffering from both the rugged trail conditions and rheumatism, he headed back down the trail and home to California. It must have been a heartbreaking decision for him as he had mortgaged his home to underwrite the journey for one last big adventure. Now the dream was gone.

His replacement would be sixty-six-year-old Martin Tarwater, a father of nine, who came ashore at Dyea two days later. In London's short story "Like Argus of Ancient Times," there is a description of Tarwater's arrival there: "Carrying a half-empty canvas sack of blankets and old clothes, he landed on the beach in the Klondike gold rush." Not hampered by supplies of his own, the old man agreed to help pack the camera gear of his travelling companion, photographer Frank LaRoche, and the two immediately headed up the trail. Nine miles in, they met London's group. Tarwater's timing could not have been more opportune. Fred Thompson wrote in his diary, "I find since Mr. Shepard left us, I must do the cooking, but I do not like the job, had rather pack on my back." But by the time the London group reached Sheep Camp, where they took a break, Thompson was no longer complaining about having to cook. Tarwater had agreed to take on that chore in exchange for board and passage.

In "Like Argus of Ancient Times," London has Tarwater say,

"Well then, I got a proposition, boys. You can take it or leave it, but just listen kindly to it. You're in a hurry to get in before freeze up. Half the time is wasted over the cooking by one of you that he might be puttin' in packin' an outfit. If I do the cookin' for you, you all'll be better, and that'll make you pack better. And I can pack quite a bit myself in between times, quite a bit, yes, quite a bit."

It was while the group was resting at Sheep Camp that Frank LaRoche managed to muster twenty-four stampeders for a photograph. The date was probably August 21. The forty-four-year-old LaRoche was one of the better photographers in America at that time, having earned outstanding credentials as a photographer for the United States Geological Survey. He had also taken some of the most detailed telescopic photos ever made of the transit of the planet Mercury, and was a charter member of the prestigious Isaac Walton Society. When the Klondike stampede began, his goal was to photograph as much of it as he could, and he made at least five voyages between Seattle and the Alaska ports in order to portray the men and women going over the Chilkoot and White passes.

LaRoche's photo of the group at Sheep Camp, however, was probably the most important one he ever made, at least from a celebrity standpoint, but apparently he never learned he had recorded Jack London on camera—the only photo that has ever surfaced of the author's Klondike experience. In fact, London's whole group, including Tarwater, were all in the photo.

In later years London once posed in gold rush garb with a fake backdrop for a publicity shot he readily acknowledged was not taken in the north. Presumably, he would have desired the real thing for lending authenticity to his narratives. One other photo regularly appears in various references to Jack as having been taken in the Klondike. This displays London in a parka wearing a toque while standing in the snow. A dog team is in

Previous pages: Sheep Camp, Alaska, August 1897. On page 64, eighth from left, is Will Harrington, a friend of Jack London. Page 65, from left: Jim Goodman, Jack London, Martin Tarwater (with face partially obscured by unknown man), Dan Goodman and Fred Thompson. The men at right were probably Tlinglits hired by Fred and Jim to tote supplies to the top of the pass. *University of Washington Libraries, Special Collections, LaRoche 2033*

front of him. There is no question the snow and team are legitimate, but if viewers look closely they will discern that the photograph could not have been taken in the Klondike. Jack is much too old: the photo was not taken in the Klondike when Jack was twenty-one, but in Truckee, California, when he was in his late thirties!

As far as I can discern through years of painstaking research, the Alaska photo taken by Frank LaRoche is the only one ever taken of Jack on his trip to the goldfields.

Finding a photograph that one surmises London appeared in was one thing, but proving it was another. But comparing dates from Fred Thompson's diary (provided by London scholar King Hendricks of Utah State University) to records of LaRoche's own movements through the Klondike, positively identifying other figures in the photo including Jim Goodman, Fred Thompson, Martin Tarwater and celebrated missionary and author Samuel Hall Young, and favourably comparing London's appearance, clothing and stance to other photographs and descriptions of London (including a detailed study by identification expert David Sills of the Toronto Police Department) all provided sound evidence that the figure in LaRoche's photo could be none other than our "sailor on snowshoes."

In addition, LaRoche's picture illustrates the hardships endured on the trail better than words could. It is taken looking

London poses in northern garb in Truckee, California, nearly twenty years after the Sheep Camp photograph. *Courtesy of the Bancroft Library, University of California, Berkeley*

Comparing known photos of Jack London and those in his party to the Sheep Camp photo confirms that LaRoche did in fact photograph the writer as a young man. Left: London five years after his return from the Klondike. Right: Will Harrington, as an older man, identified in the LaRoche photo by his grandson Al Voris. *Courtesy London Estate and Al Voris*

downhill with a glacier in the background. The men are a sombre bunch. Not one is smiling. It is August yet all are wearing coats and sweaters, and they are standing in mud. The conditions are fully supported by Fred Thompson's diary entry on the place: "Sheep Camp is a very tough hole. Rain Aug. 23 and, oh, the mud. Moved quite a distance [300 yards] above Sheep Camp. Trail very bad, are getting up pretty close to snow. It is quite cold tonight."

The rain Thompson complained about in his diary was incessant over the next seven days, moving him to comment, "August 30, rain and wind on summit very bad. Made two trips and moved our camp to the foot of the summit where we camped on the cold rocks with ice cold water running underneath them.

Gathered what brush and moss we could find and spread it on our rocky floor in tent. Ate our scanty supper and we had barely wood enough to get breakfast with as we had to pack it two miles. Spread our blankets and tried to get some sleep on the soft side of many sharp stones."

London's own view of the final ascent of Chilkoot Pass was included in his first novel, *A Daughter of the Snows*, published in 1902. Though the plot of this book is thin, his description is superb. He wrote, "On either hand rose the ice-marred ribs of earth, naked and strenuous in their nakedness. Above towered storm-beaten Chilkoot. Up its gaunt and ragged front crawled a slender string of men. But it was an endless string. It came out of the last fringe of dwarfed shrub below, and drew a black line across a dazzling stretch of ice, and filed past…and it went on, up the pitch…growing fainter and smaller, till it squirmed and twisted like a column of ants and vanished over the crest of the pass."

When he and his companions reached the top of the pass for the last time, it was almost an anticlimax as they had ascended it over and over again while relaying their supplies. But from here on the journey was going to be easier as most of the next sixteen miles was downhill, and since the last mile-long slope was covered with snow, they were able to drag their supplies on a makeshift "sled" made from a simple piece of canvas. Ahead were four lakes—Crater, Long, Deep and Lindeman—lying in a line before they reached Lake Bennett. At Crater Lake they had the choice of skirting the lake, which ran lengthwise along the trail, or hiring a boat. Fred Thompson reported that his group chipped in thirty dollars to ferry their supplies, thus avoiding three miles of backpacking. Then, once again shouldering their loads, they staggered along the trail beside the stream connecting Crater Lake to Long Lake. Here they were brushed by rain—and snow.

Miners and prospectors ascended the Chilcoot pass, relaying supplies
"like a column of ants." *Library and Archives Canada / E.A. Hegg / C-005142*

At Happy Camp, halfway along the trail, they stopped to
rest and sort out their gear. They were now not only under a
physical strain but heavy mental anguish as well. None of them
knew how soon the interior lakes and rivers would freeze up,
so although they were almost broken by the physical travails
of their trek, they had to press on the next day to Long Lake.
This took them over a mile and a half of country that was easily the most picturesque of the entire passage between saltwater
and Lake Bennett. The path switchbacked as it climbed over the
ridge to Long Lake, and as the trail rose, the tiny, clear pothole
lakes below, framed by dwarfed spruce, presented a strikingly
tranquil picture. But London and his companions plunged on,
hypnotized by their objective—the Yukon River before freeze-
up. Later, he would remember how "men broke their hearts and
backs and wept beside the trail in sheer exhaustion."

According to Thompson, it took them four days to relay their supplies to the launching point on Long Lake. Then again handing over thirty dollars to a boatman, they loaded their gear aboard and rowed one mile to Deep Lake, which London called "a volcanic pit filled with water." Frank LaRoche was more charitable about it. "This lake is a well-known spot on the Dyea trail…. Its shores are very popular as a camping ground for miners going by the overland route…. The surroundings are barren and rocky, and in the winter months it is an extremely undesirable place to be located. But when the snow disappears before the inspiring rays of a summer sun, it is healthy, placid, and peaceful."

Past Deep Lake, London and his friends took only one day to traverse the 300-yard-long hogback to reach Lake Lindeman. There they made camp and examined their options. Should they take their chances hiking on to Bennett in the hope of finding timber and building a boat there? Or should they stay at Lindeman and search for appropriate timber? Veterans of the trail warned them the pickings were poor at both, but that timber could be found beside a nearby navigable creek flowing into the upper end of Lake Lindeman. Taking this advice, London, Goodman and Sloper, along with another group composed of Bill Odette, Dave Sullivan and Jud Hirschburg, undertook to scout for large trees. Some five miles up the unnamed creek they discovered a stand of spruce—just what they were looking for—then returned to load up with tools, go back and commence whipsawing.

Thompson and Tarwater provided food relays to the boat builders, which meant doing a ten-mile shuttle, half of it under heavy packs. Finally after several weeks of back-breaking work, the boats were completed, and Thompson, travelling the path for the last time, noted how very swift and crooked the creek was. And this observation was not idle; this stream would be

London's party made camp at Lake Lindeman, photographed by Frank LaRoche. *University of Washington Libraries, Special Collections, LaRoche 2056*

the first test of Jack London's skills with a boat in the North Country. Undoubtedly, he had talked about his abilities, but his associates, who averaged about twenty years older, probably wondered if the young sailor was as expert on the tiller as he claimed. And they worried for good reason—they were entrusting their very existence to this twenty-one-year-old.

The men lined the two boats down the shallow river for about two miles to where the water was deep enough to launch them. Then the two parties jumped into their respective craft and shoved off into the fast current. London took the tiller of the *Yukon Belle* while Thompson and Goodman were given the oars and Sloper became the bowman. Thompson, who was inclined to understatement, wrote that they experienced a very lively ride, which translates into meaning the creek was a severe challenge to London's navigation skills.

The other craft, christened the *Belle of the Yukon,* also made the journey successfully down the creek, and the two parties agreed to stick together for the remainder of the journey. When the new team reached Lake Lindeman a "splendid supper" awaited them, prepared by Mrs. Jud Hirschburg, a passenger on the *Belle of the Yukon.* This was a real celebration: they had crossed the dreaded pass, built their boat and the waterway ahead of them was still free of ice.

Jack London had often complained about being a "work beast" in some of the jobs he had held before joining the rush to the Klondike. One of them was in a laundry where he found he had been hired by a clever employer to replace two men, yet received the salary of one. However, even that work, as hard as it was, could not match the labour he had just put in crossing the Chilkoot. In this wild jaunt to the subarctic he really *was* a work beast, toting loads of up to 150 pounds in what were virtually twenty-four-hour days. No labour organization would ever have condoned what he was doing freelance—a total of seven hundred hours work in five weeks. Never again would he work that hard at physical labour.

When the short celebration drew to a close, London and his partners rowed the *Yukon Belle* to the north end of Lindeman and he walked the creek—named One Mile River by the transients—between Lindeman and Bennett to decide whether to sail it or portage. He elected to portage. Plainly, he knew his limitations as a tiller man. For $137.50 they hired packers to haul their supplies, while they dragged the boat across the land link to Bennett. Then they rowed the *Yukon Belle* to an island just offshore and made camp. There London rigged the mast, boom and sails, and his party was ready to descend the upper lakes then go on to the mighty Yukon itself.

The Bond brothers were slightly ahead of Jack London in the race to the Klondike, and when they had reached Lake

An empty boat is floated through the shallow but swift One Mile River using ropes, 1897. *University of Washington Libraries, Special Collections, LaRoche 2062*

Bennett they had not tarried long. They set out from there on September 20, but within three days they almost suffered a disaster that, in retrospect, made for a lot of "what ifs." Marshall Bond and Stanley Pearce were in one boat while Louis Bond and an individual named Virgil Moore were in a second craft. Each boat carried one of the Bonds' two dogs, Jack and Pat. When a storm blew up, the boats were caught in the middle of Marsh Lake. Luckily, Marshall Bond and Pearce were able to find refuge behind a point of land, but Louis Bond and Moore were not so fortunate and it seemed they would almost certainly drown. However, the next day the parties were reunited at the north end of the lake. In retrospect, if the Bonds and their dogs had not survived their ordeal on the lake, Jack London would never have met "Buck" and *The Call of the Wild* would not have been written.

Other characters who were to influence Jack London's work were funnelling onto the beach at Bennett around the same time. "Arizona" Charlie Meadows, a colourful fighter, cowboy, showman and prospector, had put together his own party to take a fling at the Klondike's riches. His group included another cowboy, Del Bishop, who was to become Jack London's friend. Otto Partridge also reached Bennett in September. Like the Bonds, he was from California's Santa Clara Valley and a member of the Santa Clara Fruit Growers Association. An entrepreneur, he was to remain in the Skagway–Bennett–Caribou Crossing area, and like the Bonds, he was eventually to have a tie-in with the dog of *The Call of the Wild*.

When my train stopped at the Lake Bennett station in September 1964, I wolfed down a home-style hot lunch and then sauntered across the tracks to visit the famous Bennett log church, which stood only a few yards from the lake. Only a shell remained, but it was in good shape considering over six decades had gone by since it was built by John Sinclair, a Presbyterian minister. His diocese was, in effect, the length and breadth of the railroad and must go down in history as one of the most unique congregations in North America, with the shortest time span: it almost literally began with the arrival of the first stampeders crossing the passes and ended when the railroad was completed and the use of foot and horse trails was suspended. Though rumours persisted through the years that his would-be congregation departed before he even held a service, this was not true. Sinclair actually presided here for over a year before he and his parishioners moved on, leaving only the church's shell as testimony to the restless nature of man.

I stood for a moment at the front door of the church, looking down the length of Lake Bennett, and I could understand why Reverend Sinclair chose this spot to raise his church. For sheer beauty of location, this little building ranks with any religious structure in the world.

London and his partners set out from Bennett on September 22, 1897. Thompson's spirits were lifted by the progress they were making and he wrote they were "pushed by a strong following wind and passed everything in sight." Obviously, Jack London had done a fine job of rigging the skiff, and though the three-foot waves were not easy to negotiate, his experience ensured they navigated the "high seas" without incident. Other parties were not so fortunate; many boats foundered in the tempestuous waters for lack of a navigator of London's calibre or a boat builder the likes of Merritt Sloper.

They camped at Lake Tagish that night and the next day proceeded down the lake to the strait between Tagish and Marsh lakes. Halfway through the narrow waterway, the Northwest Mounted Police had set up a customs station. According to Thompson, it took a little scheming to reduce the duty. He did

Tagish Post custom house. *Yukon Archives*

not explain how this was done, but since they had landed at Victoria on the way north, they may have claimed a high proportion of their supplies had been purchased in Canada. Their fee amounted to only $21.50. To satisfy the requirement that each man have $500 on him, there may have been some quick "loans" made between the members of their party—loans that were returned as soon as the group was out of sight of the authorities. According to Rex Kettlewell, Jim Goodman's nephew, London borrowed that amount from Goodman. Whether this was solely to get through customs or was of a more permanent nature was never clarified. After paying the fee, London, Goodman, Tarwater, Sloper and Thompson made camp on Marsh Lake, possibly close to the wide mouth of McClintock Creek. This creek mouth was so wide, in fact, that a few stampeders mistook it for the Yukon River and went up it before realizing its slow current was against rather than with their boats.

My train skirted Bennett Lake for thirty miles or so before coming to a narrow bridge that spanned the waterway connecting Tagish and Bennett lakes. Once on the other side, we were in Carcross (better known in London's day as Caribou Crossing), a tiny community huddled at the north end of the lake, where in 1900 the golden spike was driven to mark the completion of the railroad. And here, at this former hunting camp named for the thousands of ungulates migrating through the area in those days, the country opened up to a vastness that usurped all of my previous ideas of "bigness." Lakes whose shorelines disappear over the horizon, mountain ranges extending into infinity, boundless forests and eternal snowfields, all were as overwhelming individually as they were combined. It would take a towering Lemuel Gulliver to truly comprehend the enormity of this country, and in a sense, Jack London, who camped here on September 22, 1897, was that sort of a giant—albeit a literary one—because he was able to reconstruct his observations as mesmerizing dramas that would leave readers with a gut feeling for the country.

For example, the actual events that inspired London to write his short story "The League of Old Men" took place among these upper lakes of the Yukon River system—though in his story they occur at Lake Laberge. His fictional "league" is composed of a number of Native people bent on revenge for the white man's cultural transgressions, and he tells their story through the testimony given in court by an old Native after his arrest for killing innumerable gold rush stampeders. The old man, who can neither read nor write English, speaks through an interpreter in his own simplistic but eloquent defence. He says that he does not understand what is so bad about killing white men when they have invaded his hunting grounds to harvest his moose, trap his beaver, steal his women and gun down his fellow hunters. In presenting the case from the point of view of the accused,

London plumbs the depths of the desperate abyss into which the unsophisticated aboriginals fell when overrun by the whites. It is the writing of a man ahead of his time, and shatters the notion that Jack was prejudiced against First Nations people.

But like most of London's fiction, "The League of Old Men" was not solely the product of his fertile imagination. An incident of similar nature was also related to me by a Native named Johnny Joe. When I last interviewed him in the late 1980s, Johnny was almost a hundred years old, bent like a sagging tree, his legs bowed. The once-rugged body that had roamed the headwaters of the Yukon River was withered like a dried-up cranberry yet his eyes, amid the lines etched deep into his face, were still young. They gleamed and twinkled and I felt they had been that way since they first saw the light of day. His intrinsic humour had carried him through a life that had seen its share of tragedy, including the flu epidemic of 1918 that virtually wiped out his village at the mouth of McClintock Creek as well as the event that had probably inspired London's short story.

Johnny Joe's neighbours were the four Nantuck brothers who hunted and fished in the region that extended to the headwaters of McClintock Creek and then around Cap Mountain to the shores of Lake Laberge. Fish were plentiful then. Salmon ran up the Yukon River to spawn in the creek and the forests were prolific with wildlife. Then the white men came, many of them totally ignorant of Native culture, and one day the seemingly inevitable incident occurred: two white men, hunting about ten miles up McClintock Creek, were fired upon from shore by the Nantuck brothers. One of the whites was killed in the first volley, his limp body falling out of the boat. The other, seriously wounded, managed to paddle to the far side of the creek and make his way back to the hamlet at the creek's mouth, where a white trader tended to his wounds and saved his life. The Northwest Mounted Police were called in and, thanks to a tip from

Johnny Joe experienced the event that inspired London's short story "The League of Old Men."

the trader at Lake Laberge, tracked down the four brothers and brought them to justice.

The fact that Jack London was present in the Yukon Territory when the trial of the Nantuck brothers took place adds credence to the speculation "The League of Old Men" was based on their story, though nowhere in his tale are they mentioned by name. However, the plight of Natives in general can be seen in all the newspaper articles covering the trial of the brothers at the time, as well as in the records of the court proceedings. Under questioning, one of the brothers explained through an interpreter that they were taking revenge for previous sufferings at the hands of the whites. They were simply following the custom among their people that required the perpetrator of an injustice to pay for it by giving blankets, furs and so on to the offended party. If the offender failed to do so, he was annihilated by the victim's relatives. But the Nantucks were never given a chance to elaborate on the injustices they had suffered before they were found guilty of murder and sentenced to be hanged. Later, the sentences for the two youngest brothers were reduced but both died of influenza within the year.

When the Nantucks spoke of previous wrongs, it is very possible that it was the murder of the two maternal uncles of Johnny Johns they had in mind. One of the Yukon's most successful big-game outfitters, Johns was born near Carcross in 1898, the son of a Tlingit mother and a Tagish father. While growing up he had become steeped in the lore of the country by listening to stories told by two of his uncles. One of them, Skookum Jim Mason, had guided geologists over the White Pass in the first survey commissioned by the Canadian government. Later on, he was one of the three men present when gold was discovered on Rabbit (Bonanza) Creek, a discovery that set off the Klondike gold rush. Johnny's other uncle, Tagish Charlie (not to be confused with "Dawson Charlie"), had led the first railroad surveyors over the White Pass.

In an interview with me in 1982 Johnny Johns insisted that very early in the gold rush era transgressions of the law occurred that were never reported because there were simply no law enforcement officers around. He cited the fate of his mother's two brothers in 1896. When several white men who had set up camp on the beach at the outlet of Lake Lindeman caught an Atlin Native stealing their liquor supply, they promptly shot the thief, killing him instantly. Seeing the only witnesses were two natives (who happened to be John's mother's brother's), they killed them as well. Word of the murders leaked out to the village people when the Native girlfriend of one of the whites told Johns's mother about it.

Not all of the inroads on Native culture by the whites were quite so grim. One afternoon while on a hunting trip Johnny Joe and three other villagers had stopped to lunch on rabbit stew, when under a clear blue sky the air was suddenly rent with a thunderclap. A shaman who was among the hunters rose from where he was squatting for lunch and turned to the four points of the compass muttering a prayer, a performance required by an unexplainable event. He had no sooner sat down when thunder rocked the atmosphere a second time, and again he stood up and faced the four directions while chanting a prayer. That done, he resolutely resumed his lunch. The third time the boom sounded, it was too much for the shaman. He snarled the Tlingit equivalent of "to hell with it" and refused to budge. What he didn't know was that railway construction had just reached their area, and they had just heard their first dynamite blasts.

At Carcross the railway line cuts away from the lakeshore and angles straight across country for forty miles to meet up with the Yukon River again at the city of Whitehorse, my destination. While there, when I was not covering the conference, I managed to squeeze in time to visit Miles Canyon and walk briefly along the top of the precipitous walls of this giant water chute. These natural rock bulkheads, though by that time partially flooded with water backed up behind the dam constructed below, were still frightening, though nothing like the awesome sight that had greeted London and his friends.

They reached the twin obstacle of Miles Canyon and the "mane" of the formidable White Horse Rapids on September 25, 1897, and like me, they walked the trail along the top of the canyon and carefully studied the millrace below. The walls that compressed the river into this narrow passage ranged from 50 to 150 feet in height, causing a seam or ridge of water in the middle of the river, and bystanders advised London to stick to the ridge if he wanted a successful passage. This was easier said then done, as he explained in his "Through the Rapids on the Way to the Klondike":

Our twenty-seven-foot boat was carrying over five thousand pounds in addition to human freight, and hence did not possess the buoyancy so requisite for such an undertaking.... The water, though swift, had a slick, oily appearance until we dashed into the very jaws of the box, where it instantly took on the aspect of chaos broken loose. Afraid the rowers might catch a crab or make some other disastrous fumble, I called the oars in. Then we met it on the fly...my whole energy was concentrated in keeping to the ridge.

This was serrated with stiff waves, which the boat, dead with weight could not mount. Being forced to jab her nose through at every lunge, he [Sloper, in the bow] turned and cried some warning at the top of his lungs, but it was drowned in the pandemonium of sound. The next instant we fell off the ridge...the water came inboard in all directions...I threw myself against the sweep till I could hear it cracking, while Sloper snapped his paddle short off, and as the boat caught a transverse current, it threatened to twist broadside. This would mean destruction.

However, fate swept the *Yukon Belle* atop the ridge and through a tremendous comber to plop safely right-side up in a great quarry-like, circular rock court that held a giant whirlpool. London ordered Goodman and Thompson to put out their oars and go at it, and this helped them to swirl out of the pool and into the second half of this rock-bound waterway. Again they crossed the dangerous ridge several times and then at last gently nudged the bank.

London recalled running this one-mile chute in two minutes, which meant they were travelling thirty miles an hour. Fred Thompson guessed it took them three minutes, which would have been twenty miles an hour. Experts today put their actual speed at twenty-five miles an hour, splitting the difference.

Just before London and Sloper and the others ran the canyon, a man named Joseph Rette had taken London aside and asked if he would run his boat down if he made it through all right. London could not bring himself to make the promise because Rette's craft was only a twenty-two-footer with a disproportionate load on it. However, when the man mentioned that his wife and teenaged nephew were with him, London changed his mind. He and Sloper graciously walked back the length of the trail and then successfully ran the canyon again in Rette's boat.

But the worst part of the river journey—the rapids aptly labelled the "White Horse"—was yet to come. When it became known that London and his partners had elected to run the rapids a crowd of a thousand or more spectators gathered. London knew that the White Horse Rapids were more dangerous than Miles Canyon:

> The dangerous point in these rapids is at the tail end, called "the mane of the horse" from a succession of foamy, mountainous waves.... When we struck the mane, the *Yukon Belle* forgot her heavy load, taking a series of leaps almost clear of the water, alternating with as many burials in the troughs.... I lost control.
>
> We were traveling at racehorse speed.... The *Yukon Belle* headed directly for the jagged left bank.... Like a flash I was bearing against the opposite side of the sweep. The boat answered and headed upstream...completing the circle we were thrown [again] into the mane which we shot a second time and safely ended in a friendly eddy below.

But London and Sloper were not finished yet. Again they walked back to Rette's boat and for a second time ran the dreaded rapids. He probably gave his reasons for doing this favour in his

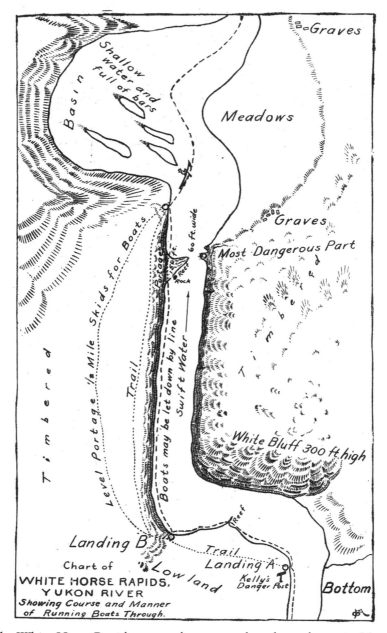

The White Horse Rapids were a dangerous obstacle, as shown in *Map Guide, Seattle to Dawson*, published in 1897. *University of Washington Libraries, Special Collections, UW16622*

book *Smoke Bellew* when he wrote, "After running the stranger's boat through, Kit and Shorty [London and Sloper] met his wife, a slender girlish woman whose blue eyes were moist with gratitude."

Rette offered London fifty dollars for his work but London refused. However, the incident may have given rise to the rumour that for a time he earned big money running boats through the canyon and rapids. In fact, for years a historical marker posted at the canyon has incorrectly stated as much. Rumours die hard.

That night they camped at the foot of the rapids, which would eventually become the site of the city of Whitehorse.

A number of years later I met one of the last three men to run this canyon and rapids before they were blocked by dams. Not surprisingly, this individual, Amos Burg, a sturdy American of Norwegian descent, was a disciple of Jack London. In fact, in his youth Burg had been so enthralled by London's writings that he left his Oregon home at the age of sixteen with the dream of shipping out of San Francisco as an ordinary seaman. When he reached the Bay area, one of the first things he did was to head for the First and Last Chance Saloon, which he knew to be one of London's favourite hangouts. Alas, he was refused entry because he was underage.

This was the fall of 1916, so while Burg was striving to sign on any ship in order to go to sea, his hero Jack London was dying at the age of forty just across the bay in Glen Ellen. Grieved by the loss but undeterred, Burg proceeded to look for work and finally, after calling on the same steamship line twenty-one days in a row and being turned down twenty times, he was hired on as a cabin boy. It was not a seaman's job but at least he was aboard a ship. He sailed to Australia, returned, and landed employment on a freighter as an ordinary seaman. This time he shipped across the North Pacific to Japan. Coincidentally, his

Prospectors running Miles Canyon, circa 1900. *No. 143, Vogee Collection, Yukon Archives*

ship was raked by the same storm that sank the *Princess Sophia* as she waited for assistance after foundering on Vanderbilt Reef near Juneau, Alaska. Burg arrived in Japan just in time to celebrate the end of World War I by marching in a parade up the famous Ginza.

Where Jack London focused on writing, Burg picked up a camera. In the 1920s and '30s, by combining his talent with film and his excellent way with words, Burg became one of *National Geographic*'s leading reporters. He was the first man to shoot the Colorado River in a rubber boat and navigated all of the great North American rivers from source to mouth, most of them before they were dammed. Then, foreseeing the same fate for the Yukon River and looking for a last hurrah, Amos Burg took a canoe through the turbulent waters of Miles Canyon and White Horse Rapids, not once but twice. He made the expeditions in the company of Bill Goodlad, a former Yukon River steamboat pilot and captain, and Bill McBride, founder of the museum in Whitehorse named for him. (Fortunately, this last trip through the rapids was preserved on movie film by Yukon resident Rolf Hougen.)

Wearing "Mae West" life preservers and old clothes, the men shot this terrible stretch of wild water that had destroyed so many boats in the gold rush. Goodlad compared it to riding a roller coaster, and Burg confirmed the rapids were something to be reckoned with. "Going by the crowd that turned out to watch us," he told me, "I would say taking a boat through the cataract was considered to be fairly dangerous. It was as tough a stretch of water as I have been through and on a par with the Grand Canyon, only not as long."

Ultimately, the conference I had journeyed to Whitehorse to cover for the *Alaska Empire* ended, freeing me to pursue my other plans. Nesta James, a local doctor who was returning to England for a brief training period, turned her canoe over to me to sell for her in Dawson City. A truck took the canoe up the highway to the Midway Roadhouse about 175 miles north of Whitehorse, while I took a bus, arriving there slightly ahead of the canoe.

5: DOWN RIVER

I had several hours to pass before the truck would show up at Midway with the canoe, and I spent some of this time in conversation with Eric Brown, who was using a backhoe to dig a cesspool for the roadhouse. It was late September, the time when the notorious blackfly emerges to exercise its mandibles on anything that breathes. The nights being so chilly at this time of the year inspired me to suggest that the flies must be wearing fur coats.

"If they are," said Brown, "I'll start trapping them."

I took note that the flies were thickest where he was scooping fresh earth with his backhoe, and while it was an accepted hazard of the trade for him to suffer their tormenting assaults, there was no need for me to cower before their depredations. When I moved inside the roadhouse, owner Hazel Kermode handed me a menu that proved to be a unique document indeed. It listed Deep Fried Muskrat, Side Order of Mosquito, Grizzly Steak, Fried Gopher, Ptarmigan à la Carte, Groundhog, Mooseburger, Duck Eggs, Caribou Chops and Lynx Stew. Obviously, Mrs. Kermode was way ahead of her time since her offerings predated all "roadkill" menus.

A few hours and many coffees later the White Pass truck arrived driven by George Ford, a giant of a man from Dawson City. I hopped aboard and we drove about six miles up the highway toward Dawson City before veering down a side road for half a mile or so to arrive at the downstream (north) end of the village of Minto. This tiny community was situated in a series of meadows with an open view of the river for several miles upstream. At one time it had been a thriving settlement, but was now abandoned by all but two or three families. The rest of the inhabitants had resettled where the northbound highway spans the Pelly River, a much more accessible location for trading their furs and purchasing supplies.

When a cabin was suddenly outlined in the headlights of the truck, Ford announced this was the end of the line. We unloaded the canoe, paddles and gear, then before leaving he imparted one last bit of advice: "There's no turning back here. Once you put your canoe into the water, you don't come to another road for two hundred miles, and that's in Dawson City."

No sooner had he uttered these words than the figure of a man appeared silently out of the night, though his appearance was not altogether a surprise as we had heard dogs barking nearby. The new arrival explained that he was the watchman for the vacant structure near which my gear rested and that it belonged to the Roman Catholic diocese of the town of Carmacks. Then, without further words, he turned and was gone as silently as he had come. (Cabin fever was to catch up with this watchman half a decade later, when in a deep depression he shot his wife and her sister then turned the gun on himself. Local custom dictated the destruction of his cabin, which was subsequently burned down.)

George Ford soon pulled out, leaving me to unroll my sleeping bag and crawl into it. The dogs maintained their incessant barking until they sensed no movement from my direction, then switched to a forlorn howling encompassing all of the loneliness of the night. After a long while, apparently reassured that I presented no threat to their domain, they became quiet. The moon glistened off the flow of the mighty river, its reflection creating a hypnotic effect not unlike staring into a campfire. My mind drifted.

I thought of Jack London's story "Finis"—or "Morganson's Finish" as it was first named—that was set only a few miles away from my camp immediately above the junction of the Pelly and Yukon rivers. It concerns a man who kills three wayfarers so he can have their dog team and leave the country. Eventually the lead dog from the looted team foils the thief and the man dies from starvation and the cold. The story is not one of London's best, its main fault being the lack of a clear motive on the part of the protagonist, but it was probably based on an event that took place in this same area. In the real incident, in which a crook ambushed three men and killed them, the killer's motive was clear: he wanted their gold. He was eventually caught and hanged after a fine piece of detective work by the Northwest Mounted Police.

Years later, a friend related a yarn of his own that had all of the potential of a London story and had also taken place nearby. When I met him, Brud Cyr was the head mechanic for the Yukon territorial government, but he told me about earlier days when he and his brother Laurent had cut wood for steamboats far upriver from Dawson City. He related that they were often reduced to eating rough fare and how on one occasion he had gone hunting and come back empty-handed, but Laurent had prepared some chicken that he said was "the last can." Brud found the chicken to be as tough as any he had ever consumed, and after he finished his portion Laurent informed him that he had consumed a raven!

Some time after this when the brothers were camped at

Canadian River, Brud left to go to Fort Selkirk for supplies, a distance of about seventy-eight miles. He travelled on skis and made good time but still had to camp one night on the trail, so when he reached a cabin owned by an old-timer he approached it yelling who he was and that he had met the man before. The cabin's owner, a man named Blanchard, opened the door a crack and looked him over before finally letting him in.

There were no chairs in the cabin so Brud had to sit on the floor, and there was only a tiny fire in the stove which Blanchard kept tapping with a stick. Brud also noted that two rifles had been stationed by the window and that the old man kept looking upriver. Finally, Blanchard said, "I'm looking for the man who came downriver last year and robbed my cache. I'm going to shoot him." (At this point Brud thanked his lucky stars that he had come from the other direction!)

Eventually they turned in, with Brud attempting to sleep on the floor, but he almost froze because the sourdough did not give him a blanket and he was kept awake by his host tapping the stove with his stick. Then late in the long arctic night, Brud heard Blanchard go down into his cellar in the dark and eat out of the cans of food stored there. The next day when Brud reached the trading post at Fort Selkirk, he asked the Mountie, G.I. Cameron, about the old guy. Cameron explained that Blanchard had told him about being robbed and that he had said any man who robs a cache should be shot. As Cameron had agreed with him, the old man obviously figured he had the right to shoot. The problem was he was not going to be very selective about it!

Though the motivation in London's story "Finis" was weak, his description of the cold, the wilderness, the isolation, the hardship, the frustration and the unforgiving nature of the Arctic rescues it from complete ignominy:

Then there was the cold snap. The temperature went down and down—forty, fifty, sixty degrees below zero. He had no thermometer, but this he knew by signs and natural phenomena understood by all men in that country—the crackling of water thrown on the snow, the swift sharpness of the bite of the frost and the rapidity with which his breath froze and coated the canvas walls and roof of the tent. Vainly he fought the cold and strove to maintain his watch of the bank. In his weak condition he was an easy prey, and the frost sank its teeth deep into him before he fled away to the tent and crouched by the fire. His nose and cheeks were frozen and turned black, and his left thumb had frozen inside the mitten. He concluded that he would escape with the loss of the first joint.

"Finis" was originally published in *Success* magazine in 1907 and London was paid $750, representing a 1,000-percent jump from the $7.50 he had been paid by *Overland Monthly* for "The Priestly Prerogative"—a publication he placed before he won world fame for *The Call of the Wild*. Clearly, a bestseller could make a big difference in a writer's wage scale.

The hoot of an owl brought me back to the present, and sleep finally claimed my consciousness. The next morning, thankful for the newly fallen dew that made launching easier, I slid the canoe over the grass to the Yukon River and followed that up by toting my gear and supplies. Then I carefully loaded the craft, which I christened *Chestnut* in recognition of the company that built it, placing my pack and rifle in the middle of the boat and a box of supplies immediately in front of the seat. I rolled my sleeping bag into a waterproof tarp and stowed that next to the box then ran a rope from the bow through the entire load and tied it down. If the canoe turned over, it would be to my advantage to have my gear with the canoe, not floating separately downriver or sinking to the bottom.

One last look at Minto proved rewarding. The morning sun had dissipated the river fog, leaving in its stead a mantle of moisture glistening over the tawny meadow. Breakfast smoke rose from a handful of rustic cabins. I smelled fish and noticed drying racks from which salmon hung in profusion. Frost had been nipping at the cottonwoods, alders, poplars and willows since the middle of September and the leaves reflected this change, splashing the surrounding hills with a golden hue against a background of hardy spruce trees awash in various shades of green. If there is one renewable resource of the Yukon that is undeniable, it is the gold of autumn.

Little effort was needed to launch the canoe. One shove with the paddle and *Chestnut* was afloat in the current. Travelling leisurely with nothing but my paddle and the river itself for power, I found it easy to compose subjective notes about my journey.

In beginning my trip downriver at Minto I had spared myself the rigours of Lake Laberge, which for Jack London had turned out to be almost as large a headache as Miles Canyon and the White Horse Rapids. Their first day on that thirty-mile-long lake they had faced a howling gale blowing straight out of the north. During the next two days when the wind continued to howl, they stayed off the water while behind them scores of boats were stacking up at the south end of the lake, their crews also waiting for the wind to die and worrying about freeze-up. Getting stuck on Laberge would be worse than wintering at Bennett because at least at the latter they would have been within reach of the supply points of Skagway and Dyea.

The fourth day London counselled that they start rowing, and they kept at it all day before finding a suitable harbour to spend the night. The next morning the north wind was again out in full fury, and they made only a few miles before giving up. Thompson used these idle hours to write in his diary, bragging about their boats—and presumably London as captain—when he wrote, "Our boats have made a great record and are known by everyone coming in." Finally, on October 2, they reached the northern end of Lake Laberge and entered Thirty Mile River. (The Thirty Mile is now considered part of the Yukon River.) It had taken them six days to go the length of the lake; with a favourable wind it usually took no more than twenty-four hours.

Jack London was not keeping notes, but as the man in charge of the boat he never forgot the problems he faced and he recreated them in *Smoke Bellew*—although in his novel some of the stampeders don't escape the freeze-up:

> Morning found them stationary.... A hundred yards away was the shore of the north end. Shorty [Sloper] insisted that it was the opening of the river and that he could see water. He and Kit [London] alone were able to work, and with their oars they broke the ice and forced the boat along. And at the last gasp of their strength they made the suck of the river. One look back showed them several boats which had also fought through the night and were hopelessly frozen in; then they whirled around a bend in a current running six miles an hour.

As London and his companions sailed north, the unceasing cold intensified and slush ice began flowing into the Yukon from its tributaries. They were now averaging fifty miles a day, but Fred Thompson's entry of October 3 states the case for even more haste: "About nine o'clock we all broke camp and continued our journey on down the river to about three miles below the Big Salmon River which comes in on the right, and which was throwing out considerable slush ice making it look as though we had ought to be at our destination." Shortly thereafter the weather slacked off and with it the ice buildup.

They had been warned of a "surprise approach" to Five Finger Rapids where the river runs past four rock islets splayed across the current, but they were not prepared for the suddenness of it. Thompson wrote, "In approaching these rapids the river runs for several miles in almost a circle and in case one is not posted will come up on the rapids before he is aware of it." But London followed advice to steer their craft through the right finger and had no trouble. In only a few more miles they reached Yukon Crossing, the terminus of the Dalton Trail. The entrepreneur Jack Dalton had used this trail to drive cattle from the coast to this same point, where he slaughtered the animals and rafted the meat downriver to Dawson City. Thompson noted that beef was selling here for five to seventy-five cents a pound while at Dawson City it was worth $1.00 to $1.50 a pound. London, however, was more interested in the plot value of the hard-working trail boss's butchering business, and he used it in one of his first short stories, "The Priestly Prerogative," published in July 1899. In it, the five main characters are driving dogsleds to Dawson City when three of them discover gold of a different kind:

> Many cattle had been butchered at this place...and the offal made a goodly heap. The three fellow-voyagers...gazed upon this deposit, did a little mental arithmetic, caught a certain glimpse of a bonanza, and decided to remain. And all winter they sold sacks of bones and frozen hides to famished dog-teams. It was a modest price they asked, a dollar a pound, just as it came. Six months later, when the sun came back and the Yukon awoke, they buckled on their heavy money belts and journeyed back to the south land where they yet live and lie mightily about the Klondike they never saw.

On down the river they went. The weather had turned mild and on October 6 they made sixty miles. Passing Minto, they put ashore at Fort Selkirk where there were roughly one hundred cabins clustered around a trading post. The trader had very little to sell as it had been two years since a trading boat had come this far upriver. Thompson penned his signature on the company's register, noting the *Yukon Belle* was number 4,845, but the trader informed him that there were half as many more Argonauts who had run on by without stopping.

As I paddled *Chestnut* downriver, I noted the impressive speed of the current; it took me less than five hours to cover the twenty-five miles between Minto and Fort Selkirk, where Dan Roberts, the caretaker of the old trading post there, greeted me. He was at work repairing an outboard motor.

"Commissioner Cameron told me to say hello," I said.

Roberts nodded. He had a broad, open countenance, which reflected his easygoing nature. "Come on," he said, "I'll show you around."

Only he and his wife lived at Fort Selkirk now, though in addition there were eight dogs all decidedly less hospitable than my hosts. I noted that drying salmon hung everywhere, and Roberts told me that netting salmon saved him a hundred dollars a month in feed bills for the dogs. He used these "fish burners" to run his trapline through the winter months, and according to him they were well worth the cost of their upkeep since there had been a striking increase in the price of furs. His fur crop had been a good one: the previous winter he had trapped fifty-seven lynx (or "lynk" as the trappers sometimes treat the plural), a better than average year for that particular animal.

Roberts took me through the Catholic church, which was in such good shape a service could have been held in it. The Anglican church was next on the list, and he explained that earlier that year it had been divested of a fine old pipe organ for use in another, more active place of worship. In the one-room schoolhouse, which he had attended in 1920, the original desks were still intact—kept there in readiness as though the moppets who used to attend would come again. But there were no moppets, only the gentle rustling of a few papers on the floor when a breeze swept through the open door. The school's blackboard was still in use, however. Many of the adventurers who passed through Fort Selkirk had apparently deemed it their duty to sign their names on it. Conforming, I added my name, but on a window frame as there was no room left on the blackboard.

After spending an hour at the old settlement, I bid Roberts goodbye, stepped into my canoe and again pushed off into the Yukon River. Before going out of sight, I turned and waved a paddle at him. He was still there, gazing after me—a forlorn figure. Dan Roberts was something of an anachronism, the embodiment of an era and a town that were no more. Bolstered by steamboat traffic in the wake of the gold rush, his village had boomed for a decade. Indeed, Selkirk had remained functional until the Klondike Highway had made the legendary riverboats obsolete.

Roberts generously waved in reply, and I turned and continued downriver. The cobalt blue waterway led my canoe ever northward and *Chestnut* bent to the whims of the great watercourse, allowing it to be our guide. I travelled late, eventually finding a place where a sandbar allowed an easy approach for beaching the canoe, and made camp. Placing my gear in a likely looking spot, I built a roaring fire, the kind you build for warmth and friendship and companionship. I simplified dinner by opening a can of stew and warming it next to the fire.

My cozy little camp was surrounded by giant, sweet-smelling spruce trees. The air was clear, the water was clear, my mind was clear and the friendly river churned relentlessly as its waters hastened to the distant sea. At that time of the year—late September—boat traffic was generally sparse. In fact, that year—1964—there had been hardly any river traffic at all even in the prime months of July and August, so I was guaranteed peace and quiet whether I wanted them or not. And camping alone was a fine time to cogitate on the future of the great river. My thoughts drifted back to the battle in which I was involved to save this friend from a clot in the form of a proposed dam. Some of us—like my editor, Darwin Lambert, one of the foremost preservationist writers in North America—could see no sense in the plan to build the Rampart Dam, which would block the Yukon River at its lower ramparts near Fort Yukon and flood Alaska's celebrated bird-producing area, the Yukon Flats. Even Jack London, who was never famous for testimonials on the specifics of conservation, had recognized the wonders of the bird life on those flats. And now those of us who were against the dam were finding ammunition to oppose it in an article he wrote about his trip through the flats that had been published in the *Buffalo Express*.

One pro-dam politician's riposte was that water was water, thus how could water birds be affected by a little more water? Of course, he was purposely simplifying the matter. We in return stressed the damage that flooding would cause to the wetlands—the shallow waters that are suitable only for nesting and raising the young of water birds—and the fact that in that area literally millions of our feathered friends would be displaced. Eventually, I am happy to report, the dam was defeated, though not as much by our strident opposition as by the government's lack of money.

That night, looking at the firelight reflecting off the surface of the mighty Yukon River, I found it hard to conceive just how fragile our rivers really were. But these arteries always seem to be the last to capture the public's attention, and by the time they do it is a monumental expense to clean them up. My fire was crackling and popping nicely when suddenly the noise of a large branch breaking behind my back—a noise which could only have been made by a heavy animal such as a bear or moose— caused me to whirl around and stare into the bush, the fortunes

of the Yukon River forgotten. My Winchester, parked against a tree, was a longer sprint away than the questionable sound, but it struck me that my fire would be better protection against whatever was back there, and I tossed some more spruce sticks onto it. The fire blazed up in a stream of sparks, spitting and barking like an ornery coyote, and that was when I realized the source of my worries: the cliff rising above the opposite bank—which really was not very far away—was hurling the echoes of the popping firebrands back at me. I hollered, and sure enough, my voice emerged, slightly disguised and hollow, from the bushes behind me. Old Mother Nature is always ready to be the trickster when the spirit moves her—or maybe it was just my friend the river teasing me for thinking so seriously about the future. Relieved, I rolled out my sleeping bag and drifted off to sleep.

The morning dawned

Dick North's canoe, *Chestnut*, on the Yukon River, where the canyon wall throws back impressive echoes.

cold and misty. The dew had frozen on the canoe paddles making them into smooth-surfaced icicles. Fortunately, my fire was still in a smouldering snooze and needed only a kick in the shins to get to work. Boiled Yukon River water made good tea and readied me for my next fling on the river. That day's journey proved to be educational because I met several river people including two Pelly Natives: one in his white-thatched sixties named David Silas and the other about half as old, Harry Blanchard. When I first spotted them, they were on the riverbank some quarter of a mile away. I took a kneeling position in the canoe and, paddling diagonally across the artery, gained slack water, then eased the canoe up to their raft and said hello. The older man nodded between bites on a sandwich and waved me ashore. Their raft was filled with moose meat, including a huge rack of antlers (or "horns" as they are more usually called here). Talk about hunting in the old way—these guys were doing it in spades! They had so much meat on the raft that they were sinking! In fact, they had beached it in order to add logs that would make it more seaworthy.

"We want to get one more moose," said Silas. Hunting their way was not easy. Their raft floated freely, and when they wanted to reach a likely hunting spot, Blanchard manipulated homemade oars in similarly carved oarlocks while Silas used a sweep to steer the craft. The principal problem with this technique was the difficulty of landing close to the carcass once an animal had been shot. The current, if not correctly judged, could carry the raft downstream a considerable distance, forcing the hunters to return upriver on foot for the meat.

I backed my canoe off a bit, beached it, and then joined Silas while Blanchard nailed additional cross-bracing to reinforce the raft. It was composed of about ten twelve-foot-long, six-inch-diameter logs sharpened at the heavy ends, which constituted the bow of the craft. Blanchard had prepared several more logs to

Moose hunting in the old way.

add to it but had run out of nails. Luckily, rummaging through my pack, I found a handful salvaged from the old Alaska–Juneau mine and gave them to him. They were rusty, but he said that was the way he wanted them. According to him, they would hold better than new nails.

David Silas told me he had hunted and trapped and travelled the Yukon for over fifty years. Pointing behind us, he said there was a cabin a few hundred yards back from the river. It had belonged to a man named Hansen, now dead. "A prospector," he said. The three of us walked to the cabin to take a look at it. The front door was hooked up with wire and easily opened. Inside, the cabin was in first-class condition. There were two cots with springs and mattresses, a good stove, a Coleman lantern and other basic necessities of a liveable camp. Hansen would never return, but his shack was ready for the next prospector to come by and fill his shoes—though the average river traveller would never see it because it was out of sight from the waterway.

We returned to the river, where the hunters boarded their raft and shoved off into the current. Then, only pausing to snap a picture, I launched my own craft and followed my new acquaintances as far as Kirkman Creek, where fate or whatever one wants to call it—maybe Jack London himself—gave me a tug on the arm in front of the Meloy place. Commissioner Cameron had told me that the Meloys, the owners of the Kirkman Creek Ranch, had gone to Idaho and would not be back—so there should not have been anyone there—but on reaching it I saw a boy run up to the ranch house and bring out an older man. They looked in my direction, but it was not in my plans to land there. The only people I wanted to visit besides Danny Roberts at Fort Selkirk was the Burian family at Stewart Island, fifty miles downriver. During my short interview with him in Whitehorse, Commissioner Cameron had said if anyone on the river knew anything about Jack London it would be the Burians. So Kirkman was not in my plans, but an impulse to stop there persisted. While this was going on in my mind, my paddle strokes were carving such a zigzag pattern in the water the people on shore must have thought the paddler was a victim of what Jack London wrote so much about—cabin fever.

When I finally decided to land I was already downriver from the ranch and I had to make a landing between sweepers, which necessitated jumping into the river waist-deep in order to pull the canoe out of the water. When one of my legs cramped up the current almost yanked me under, but regaining my footing I successfully climbed the bank then walked a hundred yards or so to the house and greeted the people. Of course, I had assumed they were the Meloys, but they turned out to be the Burians— the very family Commissioner Cameron had told me to visit at Stewart Island. If I had kept on going I would more than likely not have met them at all.

While Rudy Burian graciously retrieved my canoe, his wife Yvonne introduced me to two of their children, Linda and Ivan. She explained they had recently purchased the Kirkman place and had come upriver to move excess material back to their place at Stewart Island. They were also harvesting potatoes Jack Meloy had planted earlier in the summer.

The house was well put together. The door opened into the kitchen, in which there was a huge wood-burning range. On the right beside a string of windows that overlooked the river was the kitchen table. A bedroom extended off the far end of the kitchen, while to the left of the range was a small room harbouring a hand pump. The Burians invited me to take off my wet

Burians and their home on Stewart Island, 1964.

footgear and hang them by the stove to dry out, which I did, happy to stand next to the big range to absorb its warmth. The tea Yvonne brewed also helped to drive out the cold of the Yukon River. Later she cooked a delicious dinner of moose brisket and fresh Yukon potatoes, and when the sun settled on the rim of the earth and the Coleman lantern was lit, we talked about the country.

Rudy Burian's father had come to Canada after World War I. Both he and Clem Emminger, a prospector at Livingstone Creek and a permanent resident of Whitehorse, had fought with the Austrians in the famous battle of the Piave River in Italy where Ernest Hemingway had been wounded. The elder Burian had settled in Alberta and Rudy had journeyed north from there, met Yvonne, who was born at Stewart Island, and married her. Together they had carved a good living out of the wilderness through gold mining, trapping and freighting on the river.

When the subject of Jack London came up, Yvonne said she and her daughter Linda had just finished reading his short story "To Build a Fire," in which the main character freezes to death on the left fork of Henderson Creek. She told me that a prospector in the area insisted there was a cabin on Henderson in which Jack London had once lived, but she was not sure if he had said it was on the left or right fork of the creek. She promised to get back to me with that information if she met the prospector again.

The subject of cabin fever is always an interesting topic of conversation in the Yukon bush, and the Burians told me of a classic case that has never been resolved. It concerned one "Schnapps" Mittelhauser, who occasionally boasted about having had an audience with the Kaiser. He had come from Germany and set up shop as a trapper along the White River not too far from Stewart Island. Another man who also trapped in that general area was a lad called "The Labrador Kid," though his real name was Harry Maxwell Hanlon. The Kid's cabin was some twenty miles from Mittelhauser's. For some reason the two did not get along very well and "Schnapps," who was known to be on the cranky side, was not shy in telling people that he had it in for the Kid.

One day a friend of Hanlon's stopped by to see him, but he was not in his cabin and the visitor reported him missing. The police checked with the German trapper but he insisted he had absolutely no knowledge of the Labrador Kid's fate, and to this day it remains an Arctic mystery. Did cabin fever do Hanlon in? Was he the victim of an accident? One false step on thin ice and a trapper could disappear into the maw of a river and never be seen again. Or did he just up and leave the country unannounced? These questions have never been answered.

Another of the Burians' cabin-fever yarns concerned Clem Emminger, the elder Burian's long-time friend. Clem worked for many years in a gold mining venture with a partner named Louis Engle, but he called it quits when Engle began objecting to Clem's positioning of his coffee cup and kitchen utensils. If Clem put his coffee cup down on the table, Engle threw a fit because it was "the wrong place." Clem recognized the signs of cabin fever and pulled out before any damage was done.

No one is really completely immune to cabin fever, not even officers of the Mounted Police. The late James Mellor, the former mayor of Dawson City who had served with the Mounties in the 1920s and '30s, told me about two Mounties who got so fed up with one another when they were stationed together on the Arctic coast that one would rise in the morning, build a fire, eat his breakfast, then put the fire out and go back to bed, leaving his partner to repeat the process. Even the Meloys, the former owners of the structure we were sitting in, had a few cabin fever stories to tell, one involving Mrs. Hazel Meloy. Sometime later in the course of an interview in her home in Dawson City she told me that during the steamboat era the boats were supposed to stop at Kirkman Creek when signalled from shore. On one trip "Kid" Marion was the skipper and he either did not see the signal or ignored it. Hazel Meloy, who was a vintage markswoman in the style of Annie Oakley, got so mad she put a bullet right through the pilothouse. "Kid" Marion stopped at Kirkman that day.

When I left the Kirkman Creek Ranch early the next morning, Rudy Burian told me that he and his family were going to stay until noon digging potatoes before returning to Stewart Island. He promised that, if they caught sight of my canoe, they would pick me up canoe and all. And they did hoist me aboard their 115-hp inboard freighter just after I had passed the White River, a glacial spillway that changes the colour of the Yukon from cobalt to tan. From that point *Chestnut* and I travelled six miles in unaccustomed luxury. It was not exactly in the style of Jack London and his partners when *they* reached the island, but I was not going to quibble over that.

London's group had taken four days to make the trip from Fort Selkirk to Stewart Island because the weather had been pleasant and they had stopped to hunt along the way. They had also stopped to transfer Martin Tarwater to their sister boat, the *Belle of the Yukon*, which was continuing on to Dawson City. In London's novel *Smoke Bellew*, however, he turned these last few days of their journey into a frigid horror story: "The last night ashore was spent between the mouths of the White River and the Stewart. At daylight they found the Yukon, half a mile wide, running white from ice-wide bank to ice-rimmed bank."

The four men remaining in London's party landed on Stewart Island at the mouth of the Stewart River in good weather on October 9 and to their surprise found no one there, although it was normally such a busy place that it was generally known as "Stewart City." As early as 1883 four prospectors had arrived here by way of the Chilkoot Pass and prospected the Stewart River from its mouth upstream ninety miles to a tributary which would later be called the McQuesten River. It seems likely that some of these miners spent their winters trapping in this neighbourhood as well, because by 1885 over thirty cabins had been built on the island, both sides of Henderson Slough and along the Yukon River. These included a trading post established by the Alaska Commercial Company and run by Al Mayo, a former resident of Maine, who was in partnership with Jack McQuesten and Arthur Harper. The first miners' meeting was held at this post. As a result two men were expelled from the camp, one for trying to poison a partner, the other for stealing butter from Al Mayo. They were each allowed a sled and enough provisions to reach the coast; afterwards if either came within a range of 150 miles of Stewart Island, he could be shot on sight.

An estimated $300,000 in gold was taken out of the Stewart in those years, but when an even bigger strike was made on the Forty Mile River in 1886, most of the men in the Stewart camp including the trader moved to the new discovery. Rumours persisted, however, that colours had been found on some of the Stewart River's tributaries and on nearby Henderson Creek. In addition, some twenty-five miles farther up the Yukon from the island, the White River flowed into it on its left limit, and yarns had also circulated that tributaries of the White were laden with the yellow metal. So London and his associates were not exactly unknowing of the merits of their chosen headquarters. They immediately moved into one of the abandoned cabins built by the Alaska Commercial Company, though in Thompson's diary it was misnamed the Hudson's Bay Company. This cabin and Henderson Creek were to be the centre of most of their activities during the coming months in the Yukon wilderness, and it was

London's experiences here that generated many of his best short stories and novels.

Henderson Creek was named after Bob Henderson, who had staked discovery claims on it in 1897, only a few months before London arrived on the island. Henderson had come north in 1895 from Aspen, Colorado, where the crash of silver prices the previous year had shut down most of the mines. When he reached Sixty Mile Post south of Dawson on the Yukon River, the owner of the post, Joe Ladue, agreed to grubstake him. He set out for Indian River then crossed the mountains to Hunker Creek, eventually finding yellow sign on Gold Bottom Creek. It was while returning from this trek—going down the Klondike rather than the Indian River—that Henderson met George Carmack, who was fishing at the mouth of the Klondike, and told Carmack of the area's potential. This information led to Carmack making the big strike with his two companions, Skookum Jim Mason and Dawson Charlie, on Bonanza Creek. Henderson, disgusted with his bad luck, left the Yukon in 1898, though he returned a few years later to live in Dawson. Eventually the Canadian government, acknowledging his part in the original Klondike discovery, awarded him a two-hundred-dollar monthly pension for life.

The Burians' freighter pulled into a docking point marked by the presence of the MV *Yukon Rose*, a boat once the property of the Taylor and Drury Trading Company. The "T & D," as it was known, survived eighty years of competition with the mighty Hudson's Bay Company, but when roads and trucks finally made steamboats uneconomic, the company sold the *Rose* to the Burians.

During my years of research I had often visualized Stewart Island, and surprisingly it turned out to be fairly close to my suppositions. The "island" was in fact a group of islands—three

larger ones and a host of smaller ones—all of them formed by
Henderson Slough, into which flowed water from the Stewart River and Henderson Creek as well as backwater from the
Yukon River. The Burians' home and the old Alaska Commercial Company cabin that London and his friends used
in 1897 were on the uppermost island in the group, which,
as I expected, was covered with big, sprawling spruce trees,
lofty cottonwoods, and scrambling willows and alders. But
the Burians' house, which in my imagination had been a log
building, turned out to be a large, comfortable, wood-frame
residence. Built by the Hudson's Bay Company for its trader,
it had originally stood a long way from the river, but the fast
current of the Yukon had eaten away at its banks until, a year
before my arrival, the Burians had to jack up the house and
move it back more than fifty yards. This, I might add, was the
fate of all of the cabins from London's day that were similarly
situated. Either they were moved or they tumbled into the
river. Unfortunately most had met the latter fate. The Burians
also owned several outbuildings, including the Bay's trading
post, which had closed its doors when the steamboats stopped
running in 1956.

After unloading the family's freight, we sat down to lunch
and my host briefly sketched his winter occupation of trapping.
He explained that he ran about three hundred traps over three
lines, each of them registered with the Territorial Fish and Wildlife division in Whitehorse. He had built cabins on all his lines
as they were too far apart to make a single cabin feasible. To
make his rounds he used eight big sled dogs that broke their
own trail. Although he followed the same path every time he
went out in order to have it packed, the frequent snows often
made the going difficult. The principal animals he trapped were
marten, lynx, fox and beaver with the occasional wolf, wolverine
and ermine, and in the spring muskrat. There are also grizzlies,

coyotes, moose and caribou in the area but no snakes, racoons or possums.

In summer when the Burians were not freighting they were gold mining, even through those years when the price of gold was so low that it hardly covered the cost of operating the mine. However, they retained their properties, including one called "Sixty Pup" at the headwaters of Henderson Creek's right fork, and when the gold price went up some ten years later, they did quite well.

6: WINTERING AT STEWART ISLAND

As the whole purpose of the Yukon adventure of Jack London, Fred Thompson, Jim Goodman and Merritt Sloper was the search for gold, the first thing they did after moving into the cabin on the south end of upper Stewart Island was to dispatch their prospector Goodman to scout out the nearby creeks. It was still early October but winter was just over the horizon and there was little time to lose. In summer the limitless swamp and muskeg studded with grass hummocks make for less than ideal walking conditions. But in winter this same area is a white hell of cold and frost; in fact, weather data has established this part of the upper Yukon as one of the coldest places on the planet.

Goodman was back within a couple of days, having found colours on the left fork of Henderson Creek. This news was good enough to stir London and two other men who had joined them on the island, Charlie L. Meyers and Elam Harnish, to head out for the left fork with Goodman as their guide. Their hike was no short walk: the mouth of the creek was about four miles from the cabin, it was another seven miles to the forks and from there another two to three miles to the area on the left fork that they wanted to prospect.

Thompson did not go with the others, but his diary states that their party staked eight claims in all, four of which were likely on this expedition by Thompson, London, Meyers and Harnish. Sloper remained in camp to build a sled, and no claims were filed in his name on Henderson Creek. Since Jim Goodman's name does not appear among the applications filed either, he probably did not think the colours he had found were worth the ten-dollar fee.

Because of the huge numbers of gold seekers venturing into the Yukon District, the government had reduced claim sizes from 500 feet to 250 feet lengthwise along the projected baseline of the creek. However, each claim was still 1,000 feet wide—500 feet on each side of the baseline. The prospector used two stakes to mark his claim, one placed in the centre of the upstream end of the claim and the other in the centre of the downstream end. Since all claims were numbered from the discovery, and the discovery claim on Henderson's left fork was near its mouth, London's number fifty-four staked on October 16, 1897, would have been about two and a half miles up the left fork, or about a half mile above the first canyon on that fork. This is the only claim that Jack London is known to have staked.

Slush ice had begun to pour out of the Stewart River and into the Yukon River three days before London and his companions returned from staking claims, and Thompson, London, Harnish and Meyers decided to embark for Dawson, seventy-five miles downriver, while the Yukon was still navigable "to get news, mail, etc., and post ourselves on the country in general also to file our claims on Henderson." They spent the first night at Sixty Mile then floated downriver to within three miles of Dawson and camped again, not wanting to reach the city in the dark. The next morning they landed at Klondike City—otherwise known by the not-so-complimentary moniker Lousetown— an industrial area for the larger community. Fred Thompson's final still-surviving diary entry reads as follows: "Met Charles [Rand], Dave Sullivan, and William Odette who were in camp at Lousetown. They told me that our passenger Tarwater came very close to getting drowned crossing the Klondike River with

CLAIMS STAKED ON HENDERSON CREEK AND LEFT FORK IN FALL 1897 BY JACK LONDON AND FRIENDS

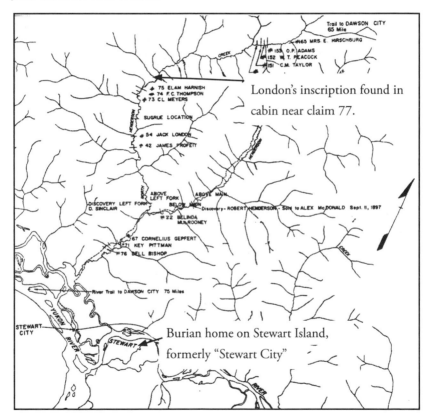

London's inscription was found in the cabin located in the vicinity of claims 75 to 79. All the points on the map were estimated from a base line survey made in 1900–1901. (Latitude N. 63°27.32', Longitude W. 139°18.70', Claim locations calculated by the author.) *Jim Leary, of the Mining Recorder's Office, Canada*

his pack on his back, and that he had gone on to Fort Yukon. Met L.W. [Louis] Bond, and we camped near Bond's cabin." The Bond brothers were sharing this cabin with their friends Stanley Pearce, Oliver P. LaFarge (destined to be vice-president of General Motors) and Lyman Colt, a rancher from Chelan, Washington, as well as the two dogs Jack and Pat.

The tent that London and his friends inhabited was not much bigger than eight feet by eleven feet. It was heated by a rectangular Yukon stove, roughly two feet by three feet, that was also used for cooking. They slept on heaps of spruce boughs on top of the bare ground—that is, if they could find any nearby. In lieu of boughs they rolled out a tarp upon which they placed their sleeping bags or blankets. There was only room for three men sleeping parallel in the back of the tent; the fourth stretched out across from the stove near the tent's entrance. A fair percentage of their budget must have gone toward firewood because they did not have a dog team to haul their own. Storing their supplies was another problem because a fair percentage of the dogs in Dawson City wandered loose when they were not in harness, and any morsel left unattended for a minute was quickly gobbled up by ever-hungry canines. As a result, the tenters became indebted to the kindness of the Bonds, who permitted them to store their staples on the roof of their cabin.

Once the weather turned cold it became considerably cheaper for the men to inhabit the bars than it was for them to remain in their tent consuming fuel. But they drifted toward the saloons as much for the company: they were warm and generally friendly places in which a man could pass hours without necessarily having to spend money. But since most of Dawson City's population in the fall of 1897 was living in tents, it was inevitable that the saloons would do a booming business.

The Bonds often invited London and his pals over to their cabin for tea or coffee, and it was on these visits that London became acquainted with Jack, the Bonds' 140-pound St. Bernard–German shepherd cross, the dog that was destined to become Buck in *The Call of the Wild*. The brothers and their friends were very much impressed by the mature manner in which London treated dogs and how the dogs responded positively. In a way he was standoffish with them, but it was this very indifference that appeared to attract them. He never fawned over them—he just sat there and they came to him. Humans responded to London in the same way.

The dog Jack was not very handsome as dogs go, but what he lacked in looks he more than made up for in heart and muscle and intelligence. One of his first jobs was to pull the Bonds' load of freight from Dawson City to Eldorado Creek, a distance of about fifteen miles uphill. The brothers had taken a lay with L.W. Fox on the Eldorado claim, and since London was a witness to the signing of that document, it seems fairly certain that he made the trip with them as he was not to leave Dawson City to return to Stewart Island until mid-December when the Yukon River froze. Thus, he would have had more than enough time to assess the qualities of the animal. Bond's diary notes, "Jack is a great worker. I have him pull a sledge load to Eldorado Creek and the next day I ride home." Bond was not nearly so complimentary toward his other dog, Pat. Of him, he wrote "Pat—the bald-faced joker we got from the expressman—is a shirk; he lets the other dogs pull him."

London's stay in Dawson City was to prove very fruitful for his fiction in other ways as well. That November the Bonds participated in a wild stampede to an unknown tributary of the Klondike River during which the temperature hit sixty below zero. Although London did not make that trip, he used the theme in several of his stories, including "Stampede to Squaw Creek." He was also in Dawson near the end of November when a jealous dance hall girl tossed a kerosene lamp at a rival. The resultant fire burned down much of the town and presumably made one grand mess in the process.

The general consensus is that at this time London also met Captain E.T. Barnette of the Alaska Commercial Company. Barnette was a thirty-four-year-old prospector, miner and promoter from Helena, Montana, who had been caught by freeze-up the previous year at Fort Yukon, situated where the Porcupine River meets the Yukon. While he was stranded there, word came that the Natives farther up the Porcupine were starving to death due to a shortage of game. Barnette and some others took food to them and the chief, John Shuman, showed his appreciation by allowing Barnette to purchase his best three sled dogs, one of them part wolf. Barnette purchased two more dogs at Circle City, 150 miles up the Yukon from Fort Yukon, to round out his team for a total cost of $1,700, and mushed them to Dawson City.

Six years later, out of London's fertile brain came the fictional account of *White Fang*, but the parallels to Barnette's account are fairly obvious. In the novel the wolf-dog is brought down the Porcupine River to Fort Yukon by his Native master, though the fictional animal is eventually sold to an ugly "bad guy" named "Beauty" Smith. If perchance London's plot did not come from meeting Barnette in person, the idea must have come from a book by Tappan Adney, *The Klondike Stampede*, that London had purchased and read. In it Adney mentions how Barnette obtained the dogs, adding, "It is the best dog team in the Klondike." He backed this up with two photos, one of a musher (Barnette) standing alone with the "wolf-dog" and the other of the whole team, of which the same "wolf-dog" is the number two from the wheel. Barnette and two others stand behind the team.

There is little doubt that when the Yukon River finally did freeze up, Jack London and his friends were ready to flee Dawson if for no other reason than to spend the winter in a cabin

Captain E.T. Barnette with his "wolf-dog." *From* The Klondike Stampede, *by Tappan Adney*

Labelled "the best dog team in the Yukon," this 1898 photograph shows Captain Barnette at left rear, and the part-wolf dog that may have been the inspiration for White Fang, second from end. *From* The Klondike Stampede, *by Tappan Adney*

rather than a tent. Before heading upriver, however, they acquired a team of dogs that were probably under the tutelage of Elam Harnish and Charlie Meyers. The trip from Dawson City to Stewart Island, using this dog team and snowshoes, took them roughly four days. That London quickly learned the physical horrors of snowshoeing while on this trip is evident from what he wrote about a similar adventure in *Burning Daylight*:

> It was a case of stubborn, unmitigated plod. A yard of pow-dery snow had to be pressed down, and the wide-webbed shoe, under a man's weight, sank a full dozen inches into the soft surface. Snowshoe work, under such conditions,

called for the use of muscles other than those used in ordinary walking.

From step to step the rising foot could not come up and forward on a slant. It had to be raised perpendicularly. When the snowshoe was pressed into the snow, its nose was confronted by a vertical wall of snow twelve inches high [after an overnight snow or on unbroken trail]. If the foot, in rising, slanted forward the slightest bit, the nose of the shoe penetrated the obstructing wall and tipped downward until the heel of the shoe struck the man's leg behind. Thus, up, straight up, twelve inches, each foot must be raised every time and all the time, ere the forward swing from the knee could begin.

It should be pointed out that when London wrote of the shoe sinking "a full dozen inches," he was describing a typical subarctic snow condition wherein the crystals are so fine there is hardly any resistance—thus the "sinking." In *Burning Daylight* he described this snow precisely when he wrote, "It was hard, and fine, and dry. It was more like sugar. Kick it, and it flew with a hissing noise like sand. There was no cohesion among the particles, and it could not be molded into snowballs. It was not composed of flakes, but of crystals—tiny geometrical frost-crystals. In truth, it was not snow, but frost."

In the short story "The White Silence" London bemoans the difficulties of breaking trail in front of the team:

And of all the heartbreaking labours, that of breaking trail is the worst.... He who tries this for the first time, if haply he avoids bringing his shoes in dangerous propinquity and measures not his length on the treacherous footing, will give up exhausted at the end of a hundred yards.... He who can keep out of the way of the dogs for a whole day may well crawl into his sleeping bag with a clear conscience and a pride which passeth all understanding; and he who travels twenty sleeps on the long trail is a man whom the gods may envy.

Though the trail-breaker made it easier for the team, if he was not in top physical condition and lagged a bit, the lead dog would often run up onto the back of his snowshoes. This usually tripped the slow mover and pitched him into the snow.

Jack London was to spend one Christmas in the Yukon, and that was at Stewart Island. He wrote two stories about it and they provide fairly good insight into what it was like to muster food and drink from a cache that was scarce in the customary refinements. That he was inspired by a tale from Tappan Adney's book is readily apparent. Adney, describing his attempt to muster a halfway decent meal at Christmas, wrote, "The outlook, therefore, was a dinner of soup, flapjacks, and beans—not even the usual 'three Bs,' bread, beans, and bacon, of Alaska fare."

In London's "A Clondyke Christmas" a nineteen-year-old stampeder, Clarence, is writing home about trying to put together a Christmas dinner from his cache of bacon, beans and bread. He sits in a ten-by-twelve-foot cabin with two bunks taking up a third of the floor space. It is eleven o'clock in the morning. Outside a pale subarctic twilight prevails while inside the only light comes from a slush lamp, a tin cup filled with bacon grease and fired by a wick made of cotton caulking.

Clarence is still trying to think of something—anything—to make this dinner special, when his brother George steps into the cabin bringing with him a rush of cold air. Clarence eyes the frost line on the door and suggests the temperature must be fifty below, but his brother, busy over the stove thawing the ice off his face, informs him the spirit thermometer registers fifteen degrees colder, minus sixty-five degrees Fahrenheit. Together the brothers run down a short list of their supplies and come up with half a cup of dried apples, enough to put two slices of apple in two lumps of dough for dumplings and leave the rest for an "apple pie." With various derivations from the three "Bs," they now have a nine-course dinner. Then while searching their cache for bacon, one of them comes up with a large can of mock-turtle soup, which adds another course. An unexpected addition arrives with two miners from Mazy May Creek who are so sick of eating moose steaks that they have brought a hundred pounds of moose in various cuts—porterhouse, tenderloin, sirloin and round—to exchange for a piece of bread. With this supply of moose meat the brothers have "trading material," and George sets off for the cabin on the next island to swap a few cuts of the meat for something tasty. He returns with a cup of dried apples and five cups of prunes. Though both are welcome additions, they still do not have the one staple that is badly needed—sugar. Providentially, another traveller just arrived from Dawson City drops in and donates two pounds of sugar and a couple of cans of condensed milk. The brothers' uncle comes by with a friend and adds a quart can of strained honey. By then the ten-by-twelve-foot cabin is crowded with no less than seven men, and Christmas dinner eventually becomes an overwhelming success.

London's second story with Christmas as a focal point involves not food but drink—which may reflect the dual nature of his own appetites. As his original partners were non-drinkers, he may have actually enjoyed his Christmas in another cabin where a celebrated punch was brewed. "To the Man on Trail" gets to the point right away. It begins with the words:

"Dump it in."

"But I say, Kid, isn't that going it a little too strong? Whiskey and alcohol's bad enough, but when it comes to brandy and pepper sauce and—"

"Dump it in. Who's making this punch, anyway?" the Kid says.

This "frightful concoction" does its work and "the men of the camps and trails unbent in its genial glow, and jest and song and tales of past adventure went round the board…. Aliens from a dozen lands, they toasted each and all. It was the Englishman, Prince, who pledged 'Uncle Sam'…the Yankee, Bettles, who drank to 'The Queen, God bless her'…and together, Savoy and Meyers, the German trader, clanged their cups to Alsace and Lorraine." London had placed many of his actual friends, only slightly disguised, into this scene, though interestingly none are his original partners—Jim Goodman, Merritt Sloper and Fred Thompson. The "Malemute Kid" was probably Elam Harnish. "Prince" was Stanley Pearce, who went to the Klondike with the Bond brothers. Bettles and Meyers were the actual names of men London either met at Stewart Island or on the Chilkoot Pass trail. And "Savoy" was Louis Savard, another prospector he encountered at Stewart.

The Malemute Kid then offers a toast: "A health to the man on trail this night, may his grub hold out; may his dogs keep their legs; may his matches never miss fire." At this point the men hear the crack of a dog whip and a musher knocks on the door and enters. London describes the man as striking and picturesque in his trail outfit of wool and fur. This newcomer is Jack Westondale, a man with three years in the country. He stays for a short nap and then takes to the trail again, obviously in a hurry. The Malemute Kid actually helps him on his way by giving him a supply of salmon eggs for his dogs. Fifteen minutes go by and a member of the North West Mounted Police shows up with his dog team and two Native special constables. The policeman says they are after Westondale, who has stolen forty thousand dollars from McFarland's saloon in Dawson City. The Mountie asks for some assistance, but at seventy-four below zero the cabin dwellers answer his request with silence. When the policeman leaves, the Kid's associates lambaste him for giving aid to a crook.

The Kid, however, explains that Westondale had entrusted his cleanup of forty thousand dollars worth of gold dust to a pal to buy claims on Dominion Creek, while he stayed behind in Circle City to care for a friend down with scurvy. His "pal," however, went into McFarland's and dropped the entire amount at the gambling tables. In return, Westondale stole what he figured was rightly his and bolted for Skagway. The last line of the story is, "'Confusion to the Mounted Police!' cried Bettles, to the crash of empty cups."

Westondale was probably based on "Klondike" Mike Mahoney, one of the great dog mushers of the day, who recalled in his book *Klondike Mike* that he had arrived at Stewart Island on December 30, 1897. He noted there were about seventy men there at the time and that one of them was a young fellow about his own age who kept him up half the night asking questions about his job as a freight and letter carrier. This youth was Jack London. As Mahoney was carrying mail as well as gold for the Alaska Commercial Company and he still had a long way to go, he declined Jack's invitation to stay for New Year's Eve. But Mahoney had made a great impression, and many of the elements of London's "To the Man on Trail" echoed the visit.

On January 5, 1898, when word spread of a big gold strike on Ten Mile Creek, a tributary of Sixty Mile River, most of London's friends and acquaintances including Jim Goodman, Fred Thompson, Merritt Sloper, Louis Savard, Emil Jensen, Del Bishop, Charlie Meyers and Louis Bond, made the fifty-mile dash from the island to Ten Mile. All of these men staked claims on the creek and went on to record them in Dawson City. Yet London, who was not the type to sit around camp very long without his persistent curiosity getting the best of him, did not take part in this significant stampede. Nor did Elam Harnish. The two men are known, however, to have taken several hunting trips together that winter, and it is possible that they were moose hunting when the news broke about Ten Mile Creek.

7: CHECKING CLAIMS IN DAWSON CITY

When I headed downriver toward Dawson City after lunching with the Burians on Stewart Island in September 1964, I had the assurance of Yvonne Burian that she would write if she found out anything more about Jack London's cabin. I paddled another fifteen miles before the sun began nicking the hills and slack water beckoned me to a mud flat on an island near Rose Butte Creek. The ground was fairly firm but as I moved my canoe, I stepped into a mudhole and went in up to my knees. Retreating from that morass, I spotted an excellent place to camp next to a stump and a pile of driftwood. With my camp made, I settled back for an evening's rest.

Experts on the subject say the best time of the year to see the northern lights is in the spring or the fall. I had seen the lights often enough before, but nothing had prepared me for the spectacle that night. When I awakened at about one in the morning, the blackness was filled with huge, wavy, blue-green-pink-tinged curtains that weaved accordion-like across the sky. And though one might expect this overwhelming manifestation of light to have been accompanied by noise, these streaks of the aurora were weaving silently in the dead of space several hundred miles up. I am aware, of course, that my "dead of space" theory may be open to challenge. In fact, I know some former residents of Whitehorse who have sworn they drove right through the northern lights one night while travelling to Carcross. And many individuals, including my wife Andrée, have attested to hearing sibilant tones as the flaming curtains rambled across the heavens. I maintain those advocates of the sound theory are standing near a formation of ice, either a lake or a river, and what they really hear is the hissing expansion and contraction of ice sheets.

After watching the "lights," I slept well for the rest of the night but woke to a thick fog in the morning and was forced to defer my journey until the fog had lifted enough for me to see my bootlaces. When at last I set out on the river again, I could hear geese honking somewhere above the fog. Finally the mist cleared, and as the sun's rays glistened off the yellow, orange and red leaves of the hardwoods interspersed with the conifers on the surrounding hills, I could see geese by the tens of thousands flying south in giant "V"s toward warmer climes. All that day and the next on the Yukon flyway, the honkers flew over in seemingly never-ending formations stretching from one horizon to the other. In the warmth of the afternoon sun I would sit in the canoe and attempt to count them but it was a hopeless task. The great flocks were everywhere, yet I found myself wondering if some day they would disappear. We take an awful lot for granted relative to our vast resources of wildlife and, as so often happens, we wake up too late to find those resources gone.

That same day I landed *Chestnut* near the Royal Canadian Mounted Police station in Dawson City, and Corporal John Boston hauled my canoe up to the barracks with his vehicle. I then hired his eight-year-old son to clean the canoe for me. (I did not learn until many years later that his fine work was offset by the fact he forgot to turn the water off and flooded his

A first glimpse of Dawson City in 1964, from the bow of *Chestnut*.

Jim Goodman, left, was part of Jack London's party. He and his brother Dan, shown in a family photograph taken around 1930, once owned the gun shop below, before they left it, stock and all, to return to California. *Right: Goodman Family. Below: Yukon Archives*

dad's basement.) My next task was to search for a place to stay. I ambled down Front Street, passing the former residence of the commissioner of the Yukon Territory, vacant since that office had long since moved to Whitehorse along with the government. I turned at the corner of Third Street where the dilapidated and unoccupied hardware store nicknamed "the gun shop" was located. Jim Goodman, who had been the hunter in Jack London's party, had once owned this handsome building along with his brother Dan. They had remained in the Yukon until 1922, by which time the local economic depression was so complete that they simply walked off and left their store, stock and all, to return to California.

Years later a rumour began circulating that during the long nights of winter the neighbours could hear a woman singing and dancing in the deserted building. When I was approached about this rumour by a lady who was recording Yukon ghost stories, I explained that Dan Goodman had brought his daughter Zella to live with them. A wonderful piano player with a voice to match, she had often entertained at the Dawson City Athletic Club and played the piano to accompany the silent movies of the day. She had gone south with her father and uncle in 1922 but she later surfaced as Dixie Lee, a popular radio personality sponsored by the Shell Oil Company. Surely, I told the lady, the ghost on the second floor of the gun shop would have to be Zella, whose piano is still in the building, albeit somewhat the worse for wear after having gone through three or four floods.

I carried on to the Occidental Hotel where the grey-haired proprietor Ole Christianson held court in a bar on whose walls rested one of the finest gun collections in the country. His wife showed me to a room in one of the trailer units located next to the hotel. Bathing long enough to drain the hotel's entire hot water supply, I dressed and headed out to look for the *Dawson News* office—or what was left of it. It had shut down in the

1950s after being in operation since 1898. I sought out Fred Caley, whom the townsfolk said owned the building, and asked him if I could look inside. His general store was right across the street from the *News,* and as he handed me a key and a flashlight he said, "I'll sell you the place if you want it."

Not having asked the owner what was left inside the building, it came as a complete surprise to find the printing equipment was still intact. In fact, even the bound volumes of all the previous editions were on hand. I pinched myself over what was there, and even today I have a hard time believing that twelve years after the paper's last edition was put out this office was virtually untouched. Staring around the "city room" and picking my way among the bound editions that were scattered about, it came to my mind there might be something in them about Jack London. What, for example, would I find if I checked an issue near the date of his death, November 22, 1916? Sure enough, there was an article about him, but in sharp contrast to the many newspapers around the world that gave London's death a banner headline, the article in the *News* was a one-column piece at the bottom of the front page. It read, "Jack London, Pioneer of the Yukon, Dead, San Francisco, Nov. 23—Jack London, noted California author, whose specialty was northern tales, died yesterday. London joined the stampede to the Klondike in the first days of the camp and spent the winter in Dawson." The concluding paragraph was a local note mentioning his connection with the city. "Jack London has not visited Dawson since the early days of the camp. When here he lived in a cabin situated on the edge of the rock slide on the north side of the city, and is remembered by many living here."

I continued to scan the back issues, though I doubted I would find anything more about him. Judging from the newspaper's content in 1916 and with the "Great War" going on at the time, I knew that the one or two writers putting out this entire daily

At centre is St. Mary's Hospital, where London was treated as an outpatient for scurvy. The Bond cabin is closest to the hospital, with a dogsled leaning against the wall. London's tent was located in approximately the same location as the white tent in the foreground. *Photograph c. 1901, Jim Robb Collection*

paper hadn't had time for leisurely profiles or lengthy feature articles. I felt fortunate to have uncovered that one article, and the mention of the cabin was like panning colours on a virgin creek. A Jack London cabin in Dawson City would be an unforeseen bonus if it could be proved he had once lived there.

I knew that London had been in Dawson City twice but the first time in December 1897 he had lived in a tent. Therefore, the cabin mentioned in the newspaper could only date to the late spring of 1898 when he was preparing to leave the north. London had developed an ugly case of scurvy near the end of his stay on Stewart Island, caused by improper nutrition. He suffered the muscular degeneration that went with that illness, his gums softened and he lost some teeth. As he was in dire need of medical attention, as soon as breakup came in 1898 he and B.F. "Doc" Harvey tore down the cabin in which they were living. Then, finding a part of a log boom that had gone astray in the breakup, they piled the cabin logs on it and floated down to Dawson City, where they sold the entire lash-up for six hundred dollars.

By this time one of London's friends, Emil Jensen, was installed in a cabin of his own in Dawson and London moved in with him in the latter part of May. The two had met at Stewart Island after London watched Jensen deftly avoid drift ice to bring a boat ashore. Jensen, who was thirty-six at the time and also from the San Francisco Bay area, recalled London as being a "curly-haired, blue-eyed boy" when they first met. Boarding at Jensen's cabin, it may be assumed London became an outpatient there at nearby St. Mary's Hospital.

When I returned the key to Mr. Caley I thanked him for the offer to sell the plant to me but turned it down due to insufficient funds. Then I hastened to Front Street and followed it to the north end of town. The day was warm and clear with pastel blue skies. The trees on the hills surrounding the city were ablaze with buttery leaves that cast an elegant glow as if the gold dug from the ground had been suddenly sprayed helter-skelter on the aspens, poplars, and willows. This was in sharp contrast to Dawson City's grey and brown buildings. Many of them were either tumbled down or twisted into odd shapes by the permafrost that squirmed beneath their foundations like some invisible leviathan pushing them around.

Jesuit priest, Father William Henry Judge. *Judge Family*

At some time in the distant past part of the mountain behind the city had sloughed off—either as the result of an earthquake or incessant rains—to create a slide, but now there were no cabins to be seen there. Instead, I found myself looking at the village dump. Any cabins that had been there in London's day had probably been torn down and the lumber used in putting up other buildings or burned as firewood. St. Mary's Hospital, which had been built in that same area through the efforts of London's friend, the Jesuit priest Father William Henry Judge, was also gone. It had burned to the ground in February 1950, and its ruins lay immediately below the staging area for the garbage trucks. The Catholic rectory was also gone, and the church had been moved to Mayo, though its steeple adorned a new building built on Dawson City's Fifth Avenue. All that was left of Father Judge's complex was a small white cottage—that may or may not have been a part of one of the original buildings—

and his grave, which I found amid a conglomeration of weeds and underbrush. Many years after my visit, Father Leo Boyd, a man possessing great perspective and a strong sense of history, had raised the funds to landscape the site and to erect a monument to the Jesuit priest. And eventually the dump was moved to a more tractable area unseen by sensitive tourists.

I continued my walkabout, leaving the north end and winding up in the Bonanza Hotel, Dawson City's oldest operating inn. The bar was a paragon of rusticity with its paintings of old Klondike scenes and people, including a fine likeness of "Klondike" Kate Rockwell, one of the outstanding actresses and singers in old Dawson and truly a pretty girl. To the right of it was a Victorian bar that had been freighted in from San Francisco. Contributing a final element to the northern atmosphere were frost heaves that made the floor look like a heavy sea in the Gulf of Alaska.

There is something about the aura of such a place that makes a beer taste better. I walked up to the bar and introduced myself to the bartender, Sid Carr, who was also the proprietor of the hotel. A man of medium height, soft-spoken and bespectacled, he had been with the Signals Platoon in World War II, had moved to the Yukon after his discharge and married a Dawson girl, Hilda McLeod, who helped him run the hotel. I told him I was retracing London's steps and that any information would be welcome. He said there was probably little information to be had around Dawson, but if there was any, the mining recorder's office was the place to go.

"Would there be anyone still alive who knew him?" I asked. This was a long shot as it was now 1964 and such an individual would have to be nearly 90 if he was around during the gold rush.

Sid Carr stared into space for a minute then nodded. "Yes, I think there's a guy in the hospital right now, but I can't think of his name. It's John something." The man's name turned out to be John Korbo, and he had been mentioned in Franklin Walker's book *Jack London and the Klondike*. Korbo had met London when a friend had called him into a bar to settle an argument with London, whom he recalled as "a pleasant chap." Unfortunately, the nurses at the hospital told me that Korbo was too ill to be interviewed.

The following day Frank McColl, the lands director for the Yukon Territory, walked me over to the mining recorder's office, which occupied a part of the post office building. There McColl introduced me to Roger Simard, the office manager, but when I told him of my mission to look up Jack London's claim, Simard asked me who Jack London was. When McColl appeared to be equally in the dark, I thought the two of them were giving me the Dawson version of a "Bronx cheer," but then realizing they were serious, it dawned on me that London might not have been as widely known as I thought. Having come from an area where his stories were required reading in school, I had assumed wrongly that everyone in North America would have read his work, which explained some of the odd looks cast my way when I had mentioned London to various Yukoners I had met. My remarks about him had rolled off them like water off a duck, the reason being they were too polite to ask who he was.

However, this state of affairs had its positive side. If London had been as widely known and had held the status in the Yukon of, say, Robert Service, composer of such delightful poems about the north as "The Cremation of Sam McGee" and "The Shooting of Dan McGrew," any structure where he had lived would more than likely have been restored long before. In fact, Service's cabin *had* been saved and was on display, and when Will Rogers, the famous cowboy film star, humorist, and philosopher, went through Dawson City shortly before his death in 1935, one of the first places the locals took him was to

Robert Service's cabin. There, Rogers signed the guest book.

Further underlining London's lack of fame, at least in the Yukon, was the fact that Roger Simard dug into the records and very shortly came up with London's original application for a mining claim, signed by him in 1897. This invaluable tract still lay where it had been deposited sixty-seven years earlier. That it had not been placed under a protective glass somewhere was, to me, little short of amazing. (At the time of this writing, London's placer claim application has been removed from the mining re-corder's office in Dawson City, but not because it received any special treatment. It and thousands of others were transferred to the Yukon Archives in Whitehorse, where anyone interested may review them.)

I realized that London's relative obscurity in the Yukon had also been reflected in the death notice in the *Dawson City News*, which I quoted earlier. Though recognizing him as a pioneer, the *News* had given only casual mention to his northland stories, again underscoring the general indifference of local residents. This being the case, my hopes rose considerably that a cabin in which he once lived might yet be found. I asked Roger Simard if he would bring out the ledger in which claims were registered, and when he did so, I began compiling a list of claims on both the left fork of Henderson Creek and the main Henderson. The ledger gave the number of each claim, the date it was staked, and who staked it, and since several hundred had been recorded, it took me two hours to copy them down. I planned to sort them out when I returned to Juneau, matching the stakers' names with my notes on the characters mentioned in London's biographical material and in his short stories—in search of insight into those he wrote about.

When I arrived at the Occidental Hotel, Bill Frazer, who was superintendent for Canadian National Telecommunications in the Yukon Territory and was in Dawson touring his

London's original 1897 application for a mining claim, signed by him at the bottom of the document (the writing at the top is that of mining recorder). *Yukon Mining Recorder's Office* company's facilities, volunteered to take Frank McColl and me up the Dempster Highway on the coming October weekend so that I could photograph the migrating caribou herd. We drove southeast twenty-five miles then turned left to follow the Dempster as it wound its way up the north fork of the Klondike River. As we approached the Ogilvie Range, its majestic spires rose in front of us like the tops of a picket fence. Snow covered the treeless upper third of the peaks with an alabaster blanket that gleamed against the background of the pale blue sky. Below the snow line the mountains were wrapped with a blood-red belt of frostbitten buck brush, and farther down, hugging the base of the cordillera, was a band of dark green spruce forest.

But description does it no justice, nor can one really lay out the depth of feeling that accompanies such a remarkable encounter with nature. The word "overwhelmed" is an understatement. Even after having been exposed to this scene again and again over a period of thirty years, I am still transfixed by the splendour of the terrain spanned by the Dempster Highway.

We climbed steadily but gradually. There were really no sharp grades until we left the timberline and ascended the brink of the pass between the north fork of the Klondike River and the source of the south fork of the Blackstone River. We proceeded down the latter to about Mile Fifty, which was the end of the road in 1964.

Bill Frazer stopped his car on the lip of an incline that was about one hundred feet above the Blackstone River. The valley below was a vibrant crawling mat of caribou, tens of thousands of them spread out in all directions, and it was one wide-eyed reporter who beheld the scene. I also noted a tent camp nearby, the white of the tent such a marked contrast to the green tundra that stretched as limitless as the huge herd. Bill and Frank explained that the owners of the tent were Loucheux, the northernmost tribe in North America. Only the Inuit reside between them and the Arctic Ocean. I learned the name *Loucheux* was given them by the French and was more a colloquial description of the epicanthic fold of their eyes than a scientific term. Anthropologists referred to them as "Kutchin," which has become Gwich'in, an Athapascan word meaning "distant people."

This brought to mind a short story Jack London wrote in which he acknowledged these people but did not give them a name. However, his references to them making war on the Pellys farther south and to the Tananas to the west leaves little doubt that he intended the people of his story to be Gwich'in. Entitled "The Law of Life," this tale concerns the abandonment of a blind old man by his son. The tribe's subsistence depends upon the skills and health of its hunters, and the old man has become too much of a non-producing burden to justify receiving a portion of their over-strained larder. He is left to his fate with just a few sticks of wood to ward off the cold, and as he waits for nature to claim his feeble body he recalls abandoning his own father long ago on the upper reaches of the Klondike— the same "upper reaches" through which I had just journeyed. London describes the weakened man's memories of burning a hole through the frozen tundra to bury a starved child and of a famine setting in during those barren years when the caribou did not come. Finally wolves, ever sensitive to weakness, close in on the frail elder to complete nature's order of things—that is, to live, procreate and die. Standing there looking down on the tent and the tundra, the hunters and the caribou, I could better sense the final minutes of the old man as London had described the scene.

But Frazer, McColl and I were not the only ones viewing that scene. Near us an artist was sitting before an easel wielding a paintbrush with hands gnarled and twisted by arthritis. I approached, requested his name and asked if I could take his picture.

"Fine," he said. His name was A.Y. Jackson, one of Canada's famous "Group of Seven," the pioneers of an art form that projected *feeling* and *emotion* more than straight illustration. He was one of the giants of his time and painted for another decade before the candle fuelling his talents finally went out.

The next day I set out for Juneau to resume my duties at the *Alaska Empire*.

8: BY DOG TEAM INTO THE WILDS

In December 1964 a letter finally arrived from Yvonne Burian. She had been in contact with a trapper named Ivor Norback, who said he and his partner Jack MacKenzie had indeed found a cabin with Jack London's name on the wall (I assumed the writing was carved into the log wall), and that MacKenzie had extracted it. However, Norback did not know the ultimate location of the slab of wood.

My hopes soared—the carving of London's name could prove to be at least some indication he had been in the cabin. Otherwise, the association between London and the cabin would be only hearsay. Mrs. Burian said she believed that MacKenzie was living at Stewart Crossing, about 220 miles north of Whitehorse on the Dawson road. Although this news was welcome, it put me to pacing the floor at night. Should I search for the cabin first and then look for MacKenzie, or the other way around? The latter seemed to be the more logical of the two, but this meant going to Stewart Crossing. Either MacKenzie was there or he was not; and he either possessed the slab of wood with London's name on it or he did not.

The cabin began to occupy my thoughts day and night. The

big problem would be getting to the area in which it stood. Having read so many of Jack London's books and being therefore imbued with northern lore, it dawned on me this project could not be pursued in any but the old-fashioned way: he had travelled by dog team and snowshoes from Dawson City to Stewart Island in 1897, and there was no reason for me not to undertake the same route using the same mode of travel. I wrote about my idea to Corporal John Boston, the NCO in charge of the Dawson City Mounted Police detachment, and he quickly replied that a Loucheux Native by the name of Joe Henry would take me by dog team any place I wanted to go. By this time I had also learned that the bus route from Whitehorse to Dawson went right by Stewart Crossing. Consequently, I could easily contact MacKenzie on my way north. Hopefully he could answer the two most important questions—one being the resting place of the slab, the other the location of the cabin.

Next came the practical considerations of organizing such a venture. Money and jobs are the bane of dreamers, but reasoning that "adventure" made good copy, I presented my plan to Darwin Lambert, editor of the *Empire*. Though he supported me and took the idea to management, they turned me down. On hearing the bad news, it occurred to me to suggest they give me a three-week leave of absence instead. Management was not in favour of that, either. But it was possible, I thought, that if I could raise funds from an outside source, my employers would be impressed enough to give me the time off. Itemizing plans and projected expenditures, I mailed a request for funds to the White Pass and Yukon Railroad. My hopes were not high since the assembled evidence was not overly convincing for a dollars-and-cents-conscious railroad. However, the idea was unique and not overly expensive.

To my infinite surprise, the railroad said yes! I later learned that this had been the result of the persuasive capabilities of Roy

Minter, at that time special assistant in charge of White Pass's public relations. He told me of his conversation with the president of White Pass, Frank Brown, a British businessman of the old school for whom public relations as we know it today was at the bottom of the list in importance. But Minter convinced his boss that putting funds back into a community for various projects was well worth the relatively minor cost. However, when it came time for Brown to sign the cheque he mumbled something like, "You're nuts, Minter, and so am I for signing this thing." Then he added, "But sometimes they work out."

In less than a month a cheque arrived in the mail and with my confidence restored by White Pass's willingness to support the expedition, back I went to the *Empire*'s management. Surely now they would at least give me a leave of absence. Again the answer was negative, though in a sense the turndown was complimentary: they said I could not be spared from my important job of covering the operations of the state government. This time, however, with my cheque from the railroad in hand, I discarded caution and gave my two weeks notice. Admittedly, I did have a fallback position: although the Alaska–Juneau Company's mine was now closed, the company had two hydro plants that supplied power to Juneau and had offered me a position as a power-plant operator.

In the meantime I wasted little time getting underway. I did not have much to pack, only winter clothes and boots, and within a week I was in Whitehorse looking for a bus to take me north. Coincidentally, Senator Bobby Kennedy was also there, fulfilling an ambition to climb the mountain newly named for his brother John. The senator was accompanied by pioneer climber and high altitude surveyor Bradford Washburn, who was mapping the mountains of the Saint Elias Range. And high overhead yet another expedition was ongoing: *Gemini 4* was spinning around the world in little over an hour for each pass.

The day after my arrival in Whitehorse, Vic Rigeler, navigator of the bus that ran between that city and Dawson, welcomed me aboard. Five hours later in Stewart Crossing, he kindly waited while I interviewed Jack MacKenzie. Stories of the trapper's strength were rife, and I knew why as soon as MacKenzie stood in the open door of his trailer. He was only about five feet nine inches, but he had broad shoulders and a barrel chest. Salt and pepper hair receded from a countenance that resembled that of actor Richard Burton. He motioned for me to come inside.

Apologizing for my sudden appearance, I quickly explained my project and straight off asked him the location of the London cabin.

"If it is still standing, about seven miles up Henderson Creek's left fork," he said and added, "You can tell it by the slash on the inside back wall."

"How about the slab of wood with London's name on it?"

MacKenzie shrugged. "I gave it to the mining recorder in Mayo, Sam Wood, but he died. Maybe his widow would know something."

After thanking the trapper for his help I got back on the bus and expressed my gratitude to the driver for waiting for me. During the rest of my trip to Dawson I pondered this new information. I knew that Jack London's stay with his original partners—Thompson, Sloper and Goodman—had not been an extended one. These men were by nature on the conservative side and may have been a bit of a damper on London's natural ebullience. His intemperate use of Sloper's axe to chop ice, thereby chipping the blade, may also have had something to with his move. But the reason may have been quite simply that there was more room in the cabin in which he next took up residence, which was occupied by E.H. Sullivan, an adventurous former judge; B.F. "Doc" Harvey, a surgeon jousting with an alcohol condition; and W.B. Hargrave, an Oregonian of about London's age.

Trapper Jack MacKenzie (above) and partner Ivor Norback (not shown), found the cabin inscribed with Jack London's name.

However, in London's written correspondence, including essays and statements from others associated with him, it becomes fairly conclusive that this was not the only cabin he lived in during the course of that winter. The question I asked myself was how many cabins had he lived in and was MacKenzie and Norback's one of them? In an article that appeared in the *San Francisco Daily News* of March 1, 1924, Emil Jensen, one of London's Klondike pals, was quoted as saying:

> Someone had reported there had been a "find" at the mouth of the Stewart River, seventy-five miles south of Dawson... we flocked there and we built cabins and dug and panned for gold with little success. But a tantalizing bit of "colour" kept showing and we stuck to the job until winter locked us in. Twenty feet from our shack, London and his partners had built their cabin. Like the others, he toiled, sweated and flung the dirt about with an enthusiasm that never diminished.

The reference to London and his partners having "built their cabin" definitely suggests a different cabin from those he lived in on Stewart Island, as both had been in existence when London arrived on the scene. On the other hand, although Jensen stated that London's cabin was "twenty feet from our shack," Jensen's claim was number sixty-seven above on main Henderson while London's only known claim was fifty-four above on Henderson's left fork. There is the chance, of course, that Jensen's quote was not transmitted accurately.

Ernest Patty, who ran a gold dredge operation on main Henderson in the late 1930s stated in his book *North Country Challenge* that a cabin in which London was supposed to have spent some time was located on the main fork of Henderson Creek. Bill Scott, who worked for Patty, confirmed this, adding that London had written a poem on the door. And, since London had gone on a big writing bender—which included many poems—before heading north, this story has some credibility. Scott claimed he and another man loaded the door onto a truck and drove it down to Stewart Landing with instructions that it be shipped to the Yukon Order of Pioneers' Museum in Dawson City. It either never arrived, or was destroyed when the museum burned down.

That the cabin MacKenzie identified was on Henderson's left fork and not the main as Jensen and Scott and Bell had suggested gave me fresh hope, because London's only registered claim had been on the left. What to do? I had made no final arrangements for the rest of the project. I could still back out and spend my time looking for the slab rather than hiring a dog team to look for the cabin. But I had to make up my mind quickly. It was already the first or second day of spring. Any more delay and there would not be enough snow or ice to make the trip, and that would mean postponing it until fall. So I scrubbed my mind of pessimistic thoughts and resolved to waste no time in obtaining a team of dogs and a guide. If several astronauts were intemperate enough to venture into space and Bobby Kennedy could engage himself in a wild whim, this itinerant newsman could certainly undertake his own caper!

I had no sooner registered at the Occidental, the hotel that had put me up the previous fall, when Constable Frank Dunn of the Royal Canadian Mounted Police dropped by with Percy Henry, who negotiated with me on behalf of his father Joe for a dog team and guide. We worked out an agreement and it was arranged that I would show up at his father's place early the next morning. Percy explained that because he had received a leg injury while logging, his brother Victor would take his place mushing the dogs. Later that night I made the usual rounds, enjoying a few beers in my hotel's bar as well as in the Penguin and the Bonanza hotels before returning to the Occidental for a good night's sleep. (Within five years all three hotels had disappeared.) The next morning found me amidst the yelping dogs and the trail paraphernalia of mushers Joe Henry, sixty-six, and his son Victor, nineteen, while they loaded their Yukon toboggan in front of Joe's house in Dawson City. Among the supplies that went onto the sled were a stove made out of an old oil drum cut in half, a nine-by-twelve-foot tent, fifty pounds of dried dog salmon, three boxes of grub and two backpacks filled with personal gear. This jumble was piled onto a tarp spread across the sled, the canvas then wrapped around the gear and tied down with a rope. Snowshoes and a rifle were tucked under the lash rope.

At this point the five four-footed canine engines were harnessed in front of the sled. The first dog, Teddy, was given the wheel position. When this dog, who weighed about seventy pounds and was about as pleasant as a starving wolverine, paused briefly for a snap at my leg, I was told that less than six months earlier he had killed a much larger dog in a fight. As he was hitched up, the other dogs strained and pulled and jumped against their chains, yelping, barking, growling, grunting and coughing in their excitement to join him.

Rover, a big beautiful malamute type, was the second dog to go into the traces. At this, the other dogs howled their discontent, afraid they would be left behind, and even with a lash rope holding the sled, the two dogs in the traces tried to jump the gun like a couple of jittery thoroughbred horses in a starting gate. They had to be forcibly restrained from tangling the traces and turning the sled over. Rover then glanced over at my 210-pound frame and the loaded sled, promptly slipped his harness and ran under the house. He was obviously a thinking man's dog. When we finally lured him out from his sanctuary and placed him into harness, he turned around and looked at me like a New York cab driver sneering at a tourist.

The third canine to take his place in the team was Scotty. A big malamute police dog cross with a rollicking personality, he was obviously a bit skeptical about the expedition. He barked a few annoyances that seemed to say, "If I have to haul this load in order to stay out of the dog pound, take me back to the pound." But all in all, Scotty was very friendly and the Henrys' personal favourite.

Fourth in line from the wheel was Rex, a full-blooded German shepherd who had been recently shipped to Dawson City from Mayo. The quiet man of the team, he kept most of his thoughts to himself and seldom barked. Probably being in line behind Rake, the lead dog, kept him at a loss for words. For a lead dog, Rake was not very handsome. One ear was flopped over. But he was intelligent, Joe said, though possibly too

Joe Henry, foreground, with Vic, dog team and sled.

intelligent because he was inclined to shirk his duties when he got the chance.

By the time Rex and Rake were put into the harness, the entire team had resigned itself to the load and yelped in unison to be on their way. After looking closely at the heavily engaged sled, this horror-struck hitchhiker wondered if he might have to walk the next hundred miles! Victor Henry pulled the knot on the snubbing rope that had held the sled, and off like a shot went the sled, straining dogs, Victor and Joe. But in their energetic haste the crew had forgotten one important thing—me! They raced down to the Yukon River then swung left along the snow road to the garbage dump. (Dawson City's dump, which was located out on the river ice in the winter, was considered to be quite efficient: when the ice went out in the spring, so did the garbage.)

I plodded after the team, only catching up when Vic halted them not too far from the dump. I hopped aboard and hung on as Vic mushed the team upriver along a snow-machine trail. It was hard-packed, and as a consequence the dogs raced along at five to six miles an hour. Unfortunately, that didn't last. At Swede Creek, the beaten trail left the Yukon River to follow the creek coming in from the west. From that point on, a trail would have to be broken through virgin snow to make it easier on the dogs, sled and passenger. The problem was that the passenger no longer held this status. My worst fears were realized when Joe handed me a pair of snowshoes. I would have to walk!

People who have not snowshoed wonder if it is difficult. In fact, the art of snowshoeing is relatively easy when conditions are favourable, but when the terrain becomes difficult, the neophyte snowshoer can run into trouble. A steep bank, an ice bridge or heavily crusted snow can give him a rough time when he is new on the webbing. On the Yukon River—or for that matter anywhere in the north country—a snowshoer soon learns to carry a staff about seven feet long. It has a number of uses, the prime one being to tamp the ice on the river when the going becomes suspicious; it gives fair warning of thin ice. The utility of such an implement also becomes apparent when ice forms on the snowshoe harness. A couple of swats with the staff will shed the ice quite nicely. If a snowshoer falls after tripping over an ice pinnacle or ridge, the staff can help him regain his footing. It is also valuable for holding him in position while he works his way down a steep bank, the same applying when he has to climb. A hiking stick has saved an occasional life on the river when a snow or ice bridge has collapsed, sending the snowshoer heading for water. Quickly extended horizontally, the stick will catch each side of a small crevasse and prevent him from going into the river. A stick can also be extended to a person who has already fallen into the water. Still another, more simple use of the staff is for taking a pot off the fire when tea is brewed. And last, but certainly not least, if a dog is contrary and yapping, the stick wielder can tap him lightly on the head to remind him of his duties.

For me snowshoeing was such an ordeal that it generated my empathy for the gold rushers when they walked over Chilkoot Pass using the famous "Chilkoot Lock Step." I found out after a while that the agony gets organized into a pattern, and each step is achieved as an entity separate from the whole. It is not how far a person goes in a day, it is that *one step* which looms the largest. And after that one step is mastered, another has to be taken and then another, on and on. Figuring 2,640 steps to a mile and roughly one hundred miles of travel in such a foot-propelled manner, my own travail consisted of 264,000 steps. By comparison, those *Gemini 4* astronauts overhead at the time not only did not walk while travelling their hundreds of thousands of miles, they even rode an elevator to get aboard their vehicle in the first place.

For the remainder of the trip my recollections are of meeting

Joe tests the ice by tamping with a staff, while Vic and the team wait.

Vic, Joe, the dogs and sled four times each day—for mid-morning tea, lunch, afternoon tea and at night camp. My speed was fifteen miles a day, averaging 1.5 miles an hour, while Joe and Vic were capable of covering thirty miles in an average effort. Besides being in poor physical shape, I was slowed by the crust on the snow as well as the warm temperatures softening it.

We camped the first night at Ensley Creek near a broken-down cabin that looked as rough as I felt. After that, camping along the Yukon winter trail was nearly always the same, with some places better than others. Joe would first look for a good place to pull off the river because it was out of the question to camp on it since the combination of ice and snow would be too cold for dogs or humans. He also looked for spruce trees with accessible limbs that would make a spruce bough tent floor as well as nearby dead trees for firewood. However, even that experienced trailsman did not always have everything available to make a perfect camp. Late in the day winter travellers cannot be unnecessarily choosy.

First step in making camp was to clear out a level space for the canvas tent. Spruce boughs were cut and placed for the floor with a small space left clear for the stove. Next came the cutting of poplars for the A-frame of the tent and a ridgepole. Then the tent was thrown over the ridgepole and stretched out to poles braced against saplings to hold the sides taut. Two thirty-inch-long green logs on which the stove would rest were cut and placed parallel one foot apart. The bottom of the drum stove had two cross braces so that the fire holder would then be flush. The stovepipes were removed from where they had been stored inside the stove and thrust up through a pipe guard, which was there to prevent the tent from burning.

Once the tent was up, Victor would go out to chop ice for water, first using a snowshoe to clear the snow from the ice. He then chained the dogs to trees around the camp and fed each of them a dried salmon. Next he tipped the sled on its side and knocked the snow off the underside so it would not freeze there during the night. In the meantime, Joe had chopped kindling and had supper ready to cook. We ate plain grub—canned stew and fried Spam at night, bacon and eggs in the morning and sandwiches for lunch. Occasionally, we munched candy bars.

The first night on the trail we chose our sleeping areas in the tent with mine being on the left side, Joe in the centre and Vic on the right. It was not planned that way, but a certain sense of order just emerges naturally when one is on the trail. The next morning we arose at dawn and Joe rekindled the fire. After breakfast he and his son emptied the stove of hot coals and repacked it on the sled along with all the rest of the gear. Joe led off by breaking trail, Vic followed with the sled and I trailed along behind.

There was plenty of time for conjecture while we mushed our way up the ice of the Yukon River. Most of all, the journey made me wonder what it would have been like in Jack London's day. My own exertions were giving me a better appreciation of what he and the other stampeders went through, and I came to realize what he meant when he wrote in *Burning Daylight* that snowshoeing was hard, monotonous work. However, it did occur to me that the trails then, with all those people using them, would have been broken and thus easier to travel. On the other hand, we were not lugging along a year's provisions!

The mild weather was advantageous inasmuch as we did not have to worry about frozen limbs or lungs, but at night a crust formed on the snow and gradually weakened during the day until the snowshoer broke through it with every step. However, there were other obstacles on the river during that spring of 1965. The ice was the worst Joe Henry had seen in thirty-five years. In December and January the temperatures had been extreme, the mercury averaging fifty-one degrees below zero in Dawson City from December 6, 1964, to January 6, 1965. This extreme cold had caused the ice to grind and push up into an eternity of ice ridges, hummocks and pinnacles wherever the main channel of the river wound. This caused us to seek sloughs where the water was less turbulent and where, as a result, the ice was smooth.

It is difficult to describe the process of navigating through ice hummocks. Of necessity, one has to be particularly careful in such areas. Frequently I would find one of my snowshoes resting on two ice pinnacles with all my weight in the middle, an easy way to break a snowshoe. In my case, because I was often several miles behind Joe and Victor, a broken snowshoe would have caused considerable inconvenience to all of us, since it is impossible to walk in deep snow without both shoes.

The story of George Ortell is a case in point. Ortell hailed from the small town of Silvy Switch, Iowa. A handsome man with a walrus moustache and a sturdy build, he arrived in the Yukon Territory a few years after London, but unlike him stayed on in the north eking out a living as a prospector, trapper, miner and guide for the Canadian Geographical Survey. By the winter of 1943, when he had been in the Yukon for more than forty years and had become an excellent all-round woodsman, a tangled web of errors resulted in Ortell going to look for a friend who was actually seeking help for him. The temperature was sixty-one below zero when Ortell set out for Mayo, the nearest town, travelling alone through heavy snow. He broke a snowshoe and then froze his hands trying to fix it. He was at the halfway point to his destination and decided to go on. It was not long before he became exhausted. He could not start a fire. He knew if he lay down, he would freeze to death. So he packed snow up to his hips and leaned back against a tree and stood there waiting for help. The hours went by: two, four, eight, ten, twelve—an entire night.

Daylight finally broke at ten and still no one came. The frost line had crept up his legs like a man burning at the stake. His feet and legs had frozen solid to the knees, but still he stood. Finally, that afternoon he was found upright against the tree—a virtual human icicle. He was rushed to the nearest hospital where they amputated his hands and legs, all to no avail. He died a victim of the elements and a twist of bad luck.

Ice ridges can also cause a snowshoer grief if by chance they are the supports for a snow bridge crossing over a void in the ice. If that void is over deep water and the unwary traveller breaks through the snow bridge, he can expect instant death in the icy depths of the river. The first few days I was a little skeptical about the so-called dangers of travelling by dogsled on the Yukon River because we were travelling over solid ice. There were no open leads in evidence, and it crossed my mind that writers like London must have dramatized such dangers in order to sell books. However, the fourth day of the trip, my outlook changed considerably. Vic suddenly hollered to Joe, who was ahead breaking trail some distance in front of the team, "I'm looking at water!" We were on a snow bridge—from which we departed with much care, and much sweat.

Rough ice means sore feet for dogs. The pads of several of the dogs bled at different times, but we always managed to reach a slough and easier going before the dogs' feet became a serious problem. The animals all worked well and held up throughout the trip, except for Rake and Rex who got sick the last day, probably from the lynx carcasses they had been fed at Stewart River. Rex had been brought up on dog food and the lynx did not agree with him. And as all the dogs had been living on one dried salmon a day, this change may also have affected Rake. The other three, Scotty, Rover and Teddy, had cast-iron stomachs. The only time Teddy's stomach failed him was on the airplane flying home from the excursion. My guess is that he was frustrated because he could not bite the plane.

When most people think of the Yukon River, they think of wolves, and it was the same with me. We did not always hear them, but we knew they were around. The second night out the dogs raised a ruckus, and the next morning we found wolf tracks. Later at Sixty-Mile Slough we encountered five dead wolves where they had been poisoned by moose bait authorized by the Yukon Game Department. The poison's effectiveness was readily apparent when we came upon the carcasses with several dead ravens scattered in plain view around them. As the wolf is synonymous with the wilderness and all that it stands for, it saddened me to see him wiped out so efficiently, but Fish and Game men point out that they are not indiscriminately wiping out all the wolves in the Yukon. They only control their numbers

The Yukon's wolf population was once controlled with the use of poison in areas where it was judged they were overly abundant, a practice that is no longer in effect.

in areas where it is judged they are overly abundant in relation to other game.

Each night after the tent was pitched and the bedding rolled out, Joe went through a little ritual to provide candlelight for our temporary haven. He split the end of a stick. Then he wrapped a small piece of paper or cardboard around a candle, joined the two ends of the paper together and jammed them into the split end. *Voila*, a thoroughly acceptable candle holder. He shoved the other end of the stick down through the spruce bough "mattress" and plunged it into the snow, then put a match to the candle, which radiated a warmth that could never be realized from a battery light.

In the candlelit tent Vic and I would sit listening to Joe relate the legends of his people. Watching him recite was like turning the clock back hundreds of years. He had a stern Native profile, yet when I looked at him closely, I could see radiance in those dark eyes and he possessed, like so many people of his race, a pleasant sense of humour. He related tales of *dinjek* the moose, *woodsik* the caribou, *neco* the fox, *sho* the bear and *netro* the wolverine. Even though the fox was given credit for great intelligence, he never seemed to be able to match the number-one antagonist of the host of players that made up the legendary dramas of Joe's tribe—the wolverine. Pound for pound this is probably the feistiest critter that walks on four feet in the animal kingdom and has even been known to scare a bear away from a kill. So, like so many inhabitants of areas bordering the territory of a formidable animal, the Gwich'in fashioned their greatest legends around him. Since Joe's brand of English was so colourful, I would be remiss if I did not tell one legend just as he told it. This one is the story of how *sho* the bear lost his tail. In Joe's words:

Neco no like *sho* because *sho* have longer tail. One day *neco* go to *sho* and tell him watch how to catch fish. He make hole in ice and put tail in water. Fish grab tail and he yank tail out of water and catch fish. He tell *sho* do same thing but wait until just right, and he will tell *sho* when to yank tail. *Sho* put his tail in hole through the ice and fish grab his tail. *Sho* asks *neco* if he can pull up tail. *Neco* say, "No, wait longer." Night coming, getting colder. *Sho* ask if he can pull tail out of hole in the ice. *Neco* say, "No, wait a little longer." *Neco* wait long time. See *sho* tail now frozen in ice. He say, "Now yank tail." *Sho* yank tail and it stay in ice. *Neco* say, "Yank again." He yank again, and tail come off. Now *neco*, he have biggest tail. *Sho* not so smart.

Joe Henry and his wife Annie were among the last North Americans to have truly followed a nomadic lifestyle. Both were born in the wilderness and for a good part of their first thirty years they wandered the watershed of the Peel River—a 100,000-square-mile area unencumbered by roads until the late 1950s. In winter they would trap and hunt since for them the two skills went together. Joe said he would go out looking for a moose and once he had killed one they would move their camp to the moose rather than the other way around. Then they would trap the area around the moose, repeating the process once they had consumed the animal.

An indication of just how nomadic the Henrys were can be seen in the birthplaces of their first five children. Ida, their eldest, first saw the light of day at Tsii huu Creek near the headwaters of the Ogilvie River. The next was Peter, who came into this world at Tuh Riih Njin or Black Water Creek, also near the source of the Ogilvie River. Percy, the third, was born at Eneelu Tsik or Little Fish Creek; Henry first saw daylight along the Blackstone River; and Edna was born by a stream called Tshoh Khah Viinjit, which is a tributary of the Rock River. Their places of birth were to result in hilarious exchanges in later life. Only recently Percy filled out a form for his pension. On reading his place of birth, the clerk asked, "What city?" "No city," said Percy. "Okay," said the clerk, "your rural route then?" "No rural route," said Percy. The clerk put down his pen. "Come on, the nearest town?" "No town," said Percy. "Where in the hell was it then?" "On creek." "Where's the creek?" "On Ogilvie River." "Where's that?" "Runs into Peel River." "Jesus, wait till I get the boss," said the clerk. And on and on it went.

All in all the Henrys had thirteen children, but the rest have more easily located birthplaces because the family moved into Moosehide in 1931 and lived there and in Dawson City. Joe and Annie had a house in Dawson City and cabins at Moosehide, Wolf Creek and along the Ogilvie River.

When we reached Sixty Mile we made camp atop a high bank in the heavy timber above the river, and the next morning we spotted a small herd of caribou. Vic slipped on his snowshoes and took off at a jog after the herd, but though he trailed them for five miles he failed to get within shooting range. The animals had ample warning of his approach as the crusted snow cracked and broke under his weight. I was salivating thinking of a caribou steak, but it was not to be on that day. Joe Henry said that in the early days this herd—sometimes called the Forty Mile Herd because that was the area of its main migration route—was so large that steamboats were sometimes held up waiting for them to swim the river. At the time we saw them the population had dwindled from a high of thirty thousand to forty thousand in the 1930s to just five hundred or so.

We reached Stewart Island about noon on March 31. Approaching from the north, we turned off the Yukon River and followed Henderson Slough then cut away from it to mush up a smaller slough to an old roadhouse where we took photos. (This roadhouse is gone now, the Burians having utilized the logs in other buildings.) We arrived at the Burians' home just in time to repair a broken harness and the sled's brake, which consisted of two bolts inserted through a board that was fastened with hinges to the back of the sled. When needed, the board was flipped down for the musher to step on and the bolts would dig into the snow.

The Burians put us up for the night in one of their cabins, but at sunrise the following day we arose to make the trip up Henderson Creek. Rudy Burian's son Robin led the way with his four-dog team made up of Stewart, a Labrador retriever, and three big huskies, Ace, Deuce and Teddy. Since the Burians ran a trapline up main Henderson, the trail was broken, and we raced the first ten miles to the forks. This made a pleasant trip for me as I rode on top of the sled's load, but once we reached the forks the unbroken snow on the left fork forced me to don snowshoes again. We followed a trail cut through the spruce a half decade earlier by the caterpillar tractors belonging to Leo Proctor, a Yukon contractor who was moving out a gold dredge that had been in operation on the right fork of Henderson Creek. Later when I talked to Frenchie Lavoie, the operator who had led the bulldozers down the left fork, he told me that he had turned down that fork by mistake. "After running up Montana Creek on the other side of Henderson Dome, I took the wrong trail. I'd meant to go by Black Hills Creek and down the right fork of Henderson [that is, the south or main Henderson], but got into the left fork and just kept going down until I hit the right fork."

As the sun edged above the trees, the day became one I will always remember in recalling the Yukon's splendour. It was crisp and clear, and the snow crystals glittered like millions of tiny clustered diamonds. As the sun climbed above the horizon, the tips of the trees and surrounding hills were tinted pink and then gold. And as it rose still higher, the sky took on a strikingly lucid blue. Such manifestations of nature are the real gold of the Yukon. They are experienced and then stowed away in a person's memory like a miser hoarding his treasures in a vault.

We stopped for lunch at one o'clock. The snow was much deeper than expected, and one of Robin's dogs, Teddy, had quit pulling and was turned out of his harness. This dog was a solid individualist. If he thought his work was too difficult, he refused to budge. Robin said that once he had even built a fire under Teddy to stir the dog to move, but in his mule-like stubbornness Teddy merely stood up, walked a few paces, and sat down again.

When we set out again after lunch Joe Henry ranged ahead, doing the tough work of breaking trail. He zigzagged right and left, looking into the occasional cabin we came across. There had been several hundred claims registered on Henderson altogether and though certainly not all of them had cabins on them, there were still plenty to investigate. However, none displayed the telltale slash on the back wall and Joe Henry returned each time to tirelessly break more trail. As the snow became deeper my strides shortened. At last I fell behind, and the two teams and their drivers went out of sight on the winding trail.

Minutes later, I slogged around a bend and saw Joe, Victor and Robin making camp by an old cabin. It faced downstream so that the streamside of the structure was about ten yards from the creek, and I saw that a shaft had been dug between the cabin site and the creek. Since we were due to make camp anyway, I could not be sure if this was *the* cabin. Robin was standing immediately in front of the structure.

"Is that it?" I asked excitedly.

"Come look for yourself," Robin answered.

I took off my snowshoes, walked up to the door and peered inside. Sure enough, on one of the logs of the back wall was the slash—the key to the search.

We had found it! It wasn't exactly Stanley finding Living-stone, but it would do. As I studied the cabin and the surrounding area, my mind was a jumble, but I knew that what had first appeared to be a lark had taken on a more serious tone. The trappers—Norback and MacKenzie—had been playing it straight but still a tremendous amount of research lay ahead. This cabin was much higher up the creek than London's claim, so what had brought him there? A moose hunt perhaps? And that he had even been in it remained to be proved because the slab had yet to found. I was assuming that London had carved his name in the log, but how would I go about ascertaining that the famous author really was the carver?

However, already there was one thing supporting the cabin's

Victor Henry examines the telltale slash on the back log wall of the cabin on Henderson Creek's left fork.

authenticity, and that was the utter isolation of the area. This upper left fork cabin was located seventeen miles from Stewart with seventy-five more to go to Dawson City. I knew there was another sixty-mile overland route, shorter than the roundabout way by river, but both courses were tough and arduous travel. Overland, a vehicle could manoeuvre as far as Grand Forks on Eldorado Creek, but from there two passes, Calder Summit and Henderson Dome, must be crossed on foot to reach the left fork of Henderson Creek. Therefore, no easy way existed to get to the cabin site other than by helicopter.

Other than the cat trail, there was no sign that anyone had been near the cabin for years. Not even a beer can marred the scene. And the cabin itself was located on the edge of open ground heavily populated with grass hummocks or *têtes de femmes* (women's heads), as the French voyageurs called them: matted chunks of grass and turf which are wide at the top, narrowing at the bottom and usually have water seepage in between. Walking on them is like walking on an assortment of giant golf tees with rubber stems; they collapse and dump the walker into the seepage's spongy contents. A swamp like this had obviously been effective in preserving the cabin as an untouched artifact in the middle of the vast Yukon wilderness.

At the same time it did look as if this left fork of the creek had seen a flash rush sometime in the past, and my research later confirmed that stampedes had occurred there in 1897–1898, 1901–1902, and 1905–1906. These, however, had been limited to a few placer operations near the mouth of the left fork, another on Emmaline Creek, a tributary of the left fork several miles up from its confluence with main Henderson Creek, and what seemed to be evidence of some diggings immediately above the first canyon where there was a group of three or four cabins on the right limit (the left side going upstream). This was the full extent of the gold-mining activity in the area.

That afternoon we proceeded to take notes on the cabin's vital statistics. The walls were made up of forty-eight logs, each thirteen feet long. The corners were a "Hudson's Bay match" or dovetail, unusual for a bush cabin. Ivor Norback later said the structure was the best-built log cabin he had ever seen in the bush as the log corners were perfectly matched and slanted so that moisture drained down and outward from every direction. The roof was composed of forty split logs with moss and dirt thrown on top of them, but the centre of the roof had partially caved in and left a pile of turf in the middle of the cabin's dirt floor. A little spruce tree sprouted from the roof. (Later, more of the roof collapsed, taking the tree with it.) The window and doorframes were set into the logs with wooden pegs. The back gable logs were also pegged and all the walls were chinked with moss. Two two-by-two-foot openings for windows were glass-less. The door was made from wood planks with cross-bracing and was four and a half feet high by two and a half feet in width. Moosehide hinges had held it up. Written in pencilled hand-writing on the door was an inscription that I thought read, "Feb. 26, 1945, going to Dawson." Beneath the inscription was one word, "miles," which I assumed referred to a distance.

Two spruce pole bunks, almost four feet wide and six feet long, stretched across the back of the cabin with half a foot of space between their ends. The position of the bunks was such that London would have had to stand and turn slightly sideways or kneel on one of the bunks in order to put his name on the log wall. The slash was on the fourth log from the top at the back of the cabin. It measured four inches wide and twelve inches long.

A Yukon stove rested on two logs immediately to the right of the door. On the right wall next to the stove we discovered an-other pencilled inscription. It read, "Everything in this cabin left here for the benefit of the travellers. Please don't take anything." An axe-hewn table, six feet in width with supports angling to the right side wall, was located between the stove and the bunk. Another table was located on the opposite side of the cabin and a shelf was built into the wall to the left of the door.

Everything was typical of the style necessitated by the long, cold winters and a lack of carpenter's implements, and it very much fit the description in London's "A Clondyke Christmas":

> It was a snug little cabin in which he sat. Built of unbarked logs, measuring not more than ten by twelve feet on the inside, and heated by a roaring Yukon stove, it seemed more home-like to him than any he had ever lived in, except of course, always the one real home. The two bunks, table and stove occupied two-thirds of the room, but every inch of space was utilized. Revolvers, rifles, hunting knives, belts and clothes, hung from three of the walls in picturesque confusion; the remaining one being hidden by a set of shelves, which held all their cooking utensils.

The next day we loaded the artifacts we had found—a shovel with a hand-hewn handle, a pancake griddle, the Yukon stove and a can of Hoppe's gun oil that we planned to present to the Dawson City Museum—onto Robin's sled and mushed down the trail toward Stewart Island. Although we were lucky to find the structure, we had neglected to bring a saw to cut cross-sections for tree-ring dating and would have to return in order to do so.

In retrospect, there is always a tendency to forget the anxieties attached to such a project. If there had been no cabin with a slash in the back wall, the research would have ended right then. But with the first step successful, I now had to think about the next step. There was plenty of time to contemplate my future research on the hour's ski-plane flight from the Burians' place to Dawson City, seventy-five miles away.

9: BACKTRACKING

Several weeks after we found the cabin and many phone calls later, I located the widow of Sam Wood, who had been the mining recorder in Mayo, Yukon Territory. Rose Wood Zeniuk, as she now was, answered my call from Merritt, British Columbia. She told me the slab was still in her possession but that London had *not* carved his name on it as I had assumed. He had *written* his name on the log with a *pencil*!

"He wrote," she said, "*Jack London, miner, author, Jan. 27, 1898,* on it." My spirits soared but ebbed a bit when she said the slab was stored in the attic of her house in Mayo. However, at least the slab still existed, and Mrs. Zeniuk, who planned to visit Mayo that summer of 1965, agreed in the interim to send me a picture of this valuable chunk of wood.

Days dragged by and a certain degree of apprehension arose on my part in fretting over whether the slab's writing would match some examples sent to me of London's hand. One was on the placer claim he had filed in Dawson City, a second was on a photo published in *Sailor on Horseback,* and a third was a cheque with London's signature sent to me by Irving Shepard, his nephew and the executor of the author's literary estate. They indicated that London's writing had been inconsistent over a span of fourteen years. In one signature the loop in the "J" was wide, while another showed the loop as elongated.

Finally the photo of the slab's signature arrived, and gathering my collection of samples and placing them before me, I timidly opened the envelope. The similarity to a game of Russian roulette was not lost on me: one glance would give a general indication whether the signature on the slab was written by the same person. If it was completely different, my hours of research would be in vain. But examining the photos did reveal similarities. The signatures were not exact reproductions of one another, but the example in *Sailor on Horseback* was very close to the one written on the cabin wall.

It now dawned on me that handwriting experts would be an essential part of the project. Jack Asher, the district attorney in Juneau, gave me the address of Donald Doud, Examiner of Questioned Documents in Chicago and Milwaukee, and I sent off enlargements of the photo of the slab. Other samples of London's writing were sent to the Royal Canadian Mounted Police in Edmonton, Alberta. The Mounties wrote back to say that there were differences, but the fact that London was probably

Cabin inscription, "Jack London, miner, author, Jan 27, 1898." *Mining Recorder, Mayo*

Jack London's autograph on a promotional photograph. *Jack London Estate*

standing when he wrote the inscription would explain some of the inconsistencies. More exemplars were needed. Doud said approximately the same thing, but he also pointed out that to prove authenticity the handwriting must be free from "unexplainable differences." The difficulty was that no other examples of London's writing on a rough-hewn log cabin wall were available for comparison!

Examining the inscription from a historical perspective revealed favourable points for its authenticity. For example, the fact that the inscription said "miner, author" was of some significance in that London certainly thought of himself as a writer before leaving for the Klondike, though few others did. He had published material in his high school newspaper, *Aegis,* prior to the Klondike trip. As well, at seventeen he had won a San Francisco *Call* competition for the best adventure story submitted. And the spring before he went to the Klondike, he had gone on a tremendous literary bender, turning out scores of articles, poems and short stories. Failure to get them into print had not deterred him from thinking of himself as a scribe. He had his hopes!

Peter Brady, who dug gold on main Henderson in 1906, and his older brother Pat, who worked the same creek starting in 1900, confirmed that when London was at Stewart Island he had not completely dismissed writing from his mind. The younger Brady recalled that a man named Tom Bell, who ran a roadhouse at the forks of Henderson Creek, told him he had met Jack London. Bell said he had never forgotten the youth because he hacked out a blaze on a nearby tree and told Bell to remember it because he would make his mark some day as a writer. And W.B. "Bert" Hargrave, who was with Jack London at Stewart, said in a letter to London's widow that London "had an admiration amounting to reverence for anyone who succeeded in getting manuscripts accepted by publishers, and I concluded, although he never admitted it to me, that he had made unsuccessful attempts in that direction."

The word "miner" was also significant. It is unlikely that a forger or even the men who knew London would have written "miner" after his name. The only one who ever really thought of him as a miner was London himself. And possibly, since "miner" preceded "author," the inscription was a play on words! His sense of humour tended to bend that way. The date, "Jan. 27, 1898," appeared to be another point in favour of the signature's authenticity because it was consistent with the months London lived on Stewart Island.

At the same time I worried about the slab itself. Supposing it did not fit the slash on the wall? In order to establish proof, I would have to obtain it and then cart it to the cabin. And there was yet another possibility for error in the cabin itself. If it was built after London left the Klondike, he could not have written his name on it. The only way to prove this one way or the other was tree-ring dating and that would mean travelling back to the cabin and cutting cross-sections so that experts could date them. If the experts said the cabin was built after 1898, my whole case would fall apart because Jack London departed the Yukon in June of that year and never returned.

Fall moved into winter and found me with commitments in Southeast Asia. As a consequence, the cabin project went into a long stall. It was not until August 1968 that time was finally available to travel back to Henderson Creek to date the cabin. During my trip downriver I visited the Burians, and young Robin Burian agreed to help out.

The day was a scorcher as we took his freight canoe and putt-putted around the south end of Stewart Island then turned up the Stewart River for a short stretch to enter Henderson Slough, which we followed until we reached the foot of the trail up main Henderson. Here, Robin installed a battery in the Ford truck he left there all year to allow quick access to the family's gold claims far up the right fork. We climbed aboard and drove as far as the forks where, since no road went up the left fork, we parked the truck and started walking. We were only halfway to the cabin when we entered a huge burn where a forest fire had swept through the country the year before. Interestingly, thousands of acres of beautiful hay had sprung up in the burned-over area. Later I learned that such a luxuriant crop often results after a spring fire because a "cool burn" does not destroy the roots.

Joe Langevin, the forest ranger for the Dawson district, had informed me that he didn't think this burn included the area of the cabin, but he was not sure, and I was very anxious. After the extensive research already carried out, it would be a hard blow to find that the old structure had burned down. As we continued up the trail, the burn seemed to go on and on, and my hopes began to diminish. To make matters worse, the temperature was in the nineties and, when the Yukon is hot, the long days tend to accentuate the heat. As well, walking through and between the grass hummocks was not my idea of a good time. But eventually we stumbled from the burned-out country, recognized landmarks, and realized we had not yet reached the location of the shack. What a relief! Finally, five hours after we left the truck, we rounded a bend and there it was, just as it had been since I last saw it three years earlier.

Tree-ring dating of log cabins is usually accomplished by boring cores, first through the logs, and then through a nearby tree that is deemed old enough to overlap the years of the logs. Then the rings in the cores are matched up. Since we did not have a borer, we sawed down a tree about twenty yards downstream from the cabin and cut off a cross-section. We did the same with several cabin logs including those located at opposite corners of the cabin. Then we loaded up our samples and set out on the return trip to Stewart Island.

Back in Whitehorse where the *Yukon Daily News* had hired me as a reporter, I contacted a friend of mine, Don Schmiege, an entomologist for the United States Forest Service, who put me in touch with an expert on tree-ring dating. H.E. "Gus" Wahlgren worked for the Forest Products Laboratory of the US Forest Service in Madison, Wisconsin, and he agreed to give it a try. I wondered if the logs would pass this trial. They looked old enough: their insides were white and bone dry, but I knew they could have been fifty years old and look the same way. I bundled them up and sent them off to him, knowing I would have to bide my time for an answer as such a scientific examination was not done in a day.

Several weeks later the whole project received a lift when Ken Shortt, publisher of the *Yukon Daily News*, handed me a letter from Russ Kingman of Wyckoff and Associates of San Francisco. They handled advertising for the Jack London Square Association, which was located on the premises of the Oakland Port Authority in Oakland, California. Russ had heard about the cabin from Jack London's daughter Joan, and he wanted to help. While we waited for authentication, we began exchanging ideas and eventually came up with a plan to restore the London cabin in an unusual way. This was to use logs from the original cabin and, by adding others, build duplicate structures the same

Tree ring dating was an essential step in confirming the age of the cabin.
Forest Products Lab of Madison, Wisconsin

size as the original, moving one to Dawson City and the other to Oakland. The logic in this enterprise was to somehow create mutual and equal tourist attractions.

Finally Wahlgren's report came in, and it was favourable. He had counted the tree rings and established the age of the living tree we had cut. Then he had looked for a pattern in the log's cross-sections to match a pattern in the tree, a process that sounds uncomplicated, but it cannot be done without a microscope and a wide-angle lens camera. What he saw by this method was a marked increase in growth rings around 1900 in the overall pattern of the tree sample that was not evident in the log rings. Said Wahlgren, "This means the cabin log would have been cut anytime between 1875 and 1900." Though not absolutely irrefutable, the evidence was good enough for the purpose of authenticating the cabin's age.

Summing up the known facts, which included the cabin's age, the similarity of the handwriting and London's history in that area, we shipped them off to officials of the Territory and to representatives of the Oakland Port Authority. After a careful study, both approved the project. The Port Authority purchased the slab of wood from Mrs. Zeniuk for five hundred dollars and then scheduled an expedition to bring the slab back to the cabin to see if it fit the slash. This would be the final test.

Using part of a seventeen-thousand-dollar contribution from the Jack London Square Merchants' Association, Russ Kingman arranged to fly the Oaklanders to Stewart River, even persuading his friend Eddie Albert, who had starred in *The Sun Also Rises* and *Green Acres*, to accompany the Oakland group. They would arrive by Great Northern Airways ski-plane in early April 1969 and then travel by dog team from Stewart River to the cabin. In the meantime I journeyed to Dawson City and hired the services of Victor Henry and his dog team and dog musher John Semple to take me once again to the left fork of Henderson Creek. I would be using ten thousand dollars of the Merchants' Association donation to hire the Burians to expertly dismantle the cabin and rebuild it as two, and to transport one of these cabins all the way to Oakland.

On March 24, 1969, we drove the dog team via truck to Grand Forks, unloaded our sled and gear and proceeded to mush up the old trail along Eldorado Creek. Unlike 1965, when the ice hummocks had stretched along the Yukon River as far as the eye could see, this trip was one of comparative luxury because three double-track motor toboggans had cut a trail through the deep snow just two days before we got there. They belonged to forest ranger Joe Langevin, Gordon Walmsley of the Northern Canada Power Commission and his wife Lorna, and Mike Senziuk of Dawson City, who had all made the grinding trip to the cabin.

Victor struck out ahead with the dogs with John Semple as the musher. I stopped to talk with miner Art Fry, a rugged former prizefighter, who was digging a shaft into bench gravels that he figured had been missed when Eldorado was mined during the gold rush. It was a cold day, but when Art came up the shaft to say hello, he was sweating. It was tough work, but he had mined the creeks of the Klondike for years and thrived on it. I asked him what he thought his chances were of finding a pay streak.

He shrugged before answering. "My guess is it's virgin ground, and if so the prospects for gold will be pretty good."

Later I heard that he dug down twenty-five feet and found a glove! Most miners would have been quite perturbed when they came across such a theory-shattering experience, but Art laughed it off and kept the glove for a historical artifact. Then he went back to the geologic maps for another try. There were few men in the Klondike with his sense of history. He had put together an invaluable collection of tapes of old-timers who had worked the creeks in the northern Yukon and specialized in learning the history of all the individual claims staked on Eldorado and Bonanza creeks.

That first day on the trail we made sixteen miles to Quartz Creek and Readford and put up in an abandoned cabin. And that night I thought back to one of the men Fry had mentioned, an Englishman named Monty Velge who travelled to the Klondike during the gold rush and remained there, one of the few who never left. I already knew some of his story from Robin Burian because as an old man Velge had lived alone on Scroggie Creek, one of the tributaries of the Stewart River. Robin told me that Velge would leave Dawson City with an outboard motor propelling his boat upstream, stopping at Stewart Island to refuel. Though determined to stick it out on his claims to the end, he eventually became too weak to start the boat's motor, and he would solicit Robin to yank the lanyard for him so he could resume his journey. Of course, going upriver, if the outboard failed him, he could always float back down to the Burians or to Dawson City. But eventually old age caught up with him and frail and tired, he was taken to the hospital where he died in the 1960s.

The next morning we began mushing up the trail at dawn. Vic and I took turns riding on the sled because the snow machines had so compacted the trail that the path was easy on the dogs—maybe too easy. They could generate a speed up to fifteen miles per hour and going downhill even more, so when we came to an incline, I hopped aboard the loaded sled for some easy travelling. Dogs have only two ways of pulling, all out or not at all. Scotty, the Henrys' lead dog who had been part of every expedition to the London cabin, needed no urging as he bolted down the slope and we soon were going close to twenty miles per hour. It is a great sensation riding behind the dogs when they are in shape and going all out. But it is also a challenge. I found myself calling out, "Okay, you fugitives from a dog pound, you think you're going to throw this old hoss off the sled, but you've got another think coming. None of you flea-bitten tail-waggers will throw me off, you hear?" The dogs were too busy pulling to answer me, but they knew what I was telling them. They just accelerated the pace a notch, like a rocket chasing across the heavens.

When John Semple noticed that the number two dog, Bear, was sloughing off, he told the dog to get with it or he'd have his hide. Bear pulled a little harder but not without first throwing a fast glance over his shoulder as if to say, "We'll see how good *you* are!" The dogs poured on the power and Pat, the wheel dog, was soon scrambling to keep the sled from catching up and running over him as we sped down the hill.

"Come on, Pat," Semple yelled. "Git up or we'll tie you out here for wolf bait." Pat heard and kept the line between the sled and his backside as taut as he could in view of the tremendous downhill speed.

Then all of a sudden we were laughing—Semple, myself, Scotty, Bear, Dupy, Mike and Pat. We were a team—men and dogs—on promenade. And everything was going well, that is, until we hit one of the fingers of glacial ice that often form on sidehills to encase a trail for a hundred yards or more. We exploded onto the ice at a ninety-degree turn in the trail with Scotty leading the team around the bend full bore. The centrifugal force was too much to overcome. The sled skidded and slid into its forward trajectory. Sled driver and passenger went into orbit with the sled slamming into a spruce tree and driver and passenger hurtling through the air on either side of the tree. It was only luck that it was not *into* the tree.

The overturned sled brought the dogs to a dead halt, but they did not let that interfere with their personal lives. Bear and

Dupy immediately jumped Scotty (who also happened to be their sire) and in the space of a few seconds a battle royal was in progress. Bear clamped his ample jaws onto Scotty's foot and would not let go. Scotty, the old warhorse, shouldered Dupy into the snow and was at the point of disciplining his son when Semple recovered from his flight and jerked Scotty away. The dog musher then ended Bear's participation in the fight by kicking him in the muzzle—the only effective method of separating the dog's jaws from Scotty's foot. After taking half an hour to untangle the team we finally proceeded on our way, though now we were handicapped with a limping leader. Such is life on the trail.

We debated briefly whether to leave Scotty in the traces or turn him loose to follow as best he could but close inspection of the wound on his foot revealed only a shallow cut, so we elected to leave him at his post as leader to see how he worked out. For a short time he galloped along on three legs, occasionally testing his foot, and it was amazing how he could maintain the pace. In fact, in the space of three days his foot had healed completely.

One thing that newcomers to dogsled travel never forget is the pungent odour supplied by the dogs answering the call of nature. When on the trail, this smell seems to permeate everything, and when a driver finally reaches his destination he smells more like a dog than a dog and has reached a point where he thinks "dog," acts "dog" and talks "dog." But these canines can be a lot of fun. When the going is good, it seems that everyone, dogs included, have a good time. A squirrel will run in front of a team and the dogs will boost their speed tremendously. Rabbits and even jays are additional inducements. Of course a larger animal such as a moose can temporarily bring the whole show to a halt when the dog team bolts across country after the creature, dragging along the sled, passenger and cursing driver.

There are plenty of occasions for humour out on the trail,

especially when it stems from another fellow's difficulty. One of the more comical of these is when a lead dog gets it into his head to go other than where his master desires. Thus, when another man's lead dog "gees" (goes left) instead of "haws" (goes right), the musher's machinations become ludicrous as he implores his dogs to turn in the correct direction. The air may be already blue with the cold, but when a musher gets finished addressing his leader under such circumstances, the air takes on a much deeper shade of blue. Still another funny scene to watch is a driver sorting out his dogs when they become entangled in a free-for-all. If a fight starts, the whole team descends into a snarling, grabbing mass of flying dog fur. The harness becomes so hopelessly entangled at times that it takes a patient man to straighten it out. The driver will often have to pick a dog up and turn him upside down and sideways to pass him through a loop of harness while unravelling the mess. While this is going on, more than likely another dog will take advantage of his position to bite a chunk out of the culprit being untangled, and the whole situation will again deteriorate into chaos. Often the driver gets right in there kicking and snarling with the dogs, and it all appears farcical— unless, of course, you are that musher. The dogs seem to enjoy the entire match. I think they like the relief from drudgery afforded by a fight, and it seems that—like youngsters—they also enjoy the fact they have given their master a little mischief to worry about.

About twelve miles after the Indian River crossing, I came to Louis Roal's abandoned acres and turned off the Dawson trail to follow a tree-lined road to the ranch, a road that looked more like the approach to a southern plantation than a subarctic farm. The buildings appeared to be in good condition and, though long unoccupied, would be an ideal destination for guided dogsled tours. I browsed around the old cabin and barn for a short time and could only wonder about the ghosts that called Roal's place home. Later, Jack MacKenzie would tell me about a strange incident that took place there in November 1939. A half-dozen trappers had descended on Roal's ranch to celebrate Christmas and New Year's, bringing with them the usual liquid refreshments hoarded for such occasions. All went well for a couple of days, then one night when the liquor had been flowing freely someone suggested an arm-wrestling contest. It finally came down to a championship bout with Jack MacKenzie facing off against a Finn named Runer West, a morose character who at times displayed a faraway look in his eyes that bordered on lunacy. He was intensely proud of his strength, and he hated to lose no matter what the form of competition.

I could visualize the scene. The stove roaring cherry red and the ice-shrouded windows reflecting the sixty below zero that awaited any human who walked out the door. The two men hunched over a table in the standard arm-wrestling position, elbow against elbow, hand against hand, summoning the strength of years in the bush. A half hour goes by and slowly, gradually, Jack MacKenzie's powerful arm presses West's downward, finally slamming the Finn's arm onto the table—though not with any glee. He has seen the murderous look in his opponent's eyes, and he senses that West will kill him. So late in the night when all are asleep, MacKenzie hooks up his dogs and mushes back to his cabin in the Black Hills.

Was MacKenzie overreacting? Not according to Ted Skonseng, a prospector and trapper who once suffered through a harrowing winter with West. Not knowing anything about the Finn, Skonseng had agreed to "go partners" with him on a trapping venture at the headwaters of the Stewart River. The only way in was by bush plane. It was not long after they settled down for the winter's trapping that Skonseng realized that his new partner was crazy. West was the stronger of the two and treated

Skonseng as a slave, ordering him to do all the chores, and when Skonseng objected West beat him with a chain. He even forcibly hitched Skonseng up to the sled, making him pull in harness with the dogs. When I asked why he did not kill West, Skonseng said he was afraid the Mounties would think he was the one that was crazy and charge him with murder. Fortunately he survived the winter but he could display the scars on his back to prove it was no dream.

Two hundred yards after taking my leave of Roal's farm, I found myself walking through a scattering of fresh moose bones intermingled with a score of wolf tracks. It was easy to see that my approach had interrupted their dinner. Wolves are big animals, and a mature male may have front paws measuring half a foot in length. Some of the larger ones top three feet in height, which is as tall as some of the smaller caribou, and their powerful jaws make them formidable predators. However, they are also quite clever and, like dogs that have been pursued by a dog catcher, they know what a rifle means. What I didn't know is whether they also know what a man-without-a-rifle means, and whether they have ever acted on this knowledge. Only the fact that this pack had recently fed helped my peace of mind.

Normally, on a trip like this Vic Henry and John Semple would have stopped for tea while they waited for me, but it was such a nice day I did not really expect this. However, noon came and there was still no sign of them, even though my view was four or five miles distant. I put my head down and plodded on. Another hour went by, and my eyes mistook a dead cottonwood for a sprig of smoke against the sky. Yet there was still no sign of my companions. Another hour passed. I reached Montana Creek and followed their trail up that stream. Now, I could see at least a mile ahead, and I was sweating, tired and hungry, but it was not until about three o'clock in the afternoon that I saw some specks approaching me from the distant upper reaches of Montana Creek. They loomed larger and finally I realized Semple was coming back to pick me up. Without a watch, he had been carried away by the speed of the team and had not noticed how much farther he had travelled than I had. I understood, however, when it is a beautiful day and the going is good, it takes a lot of willpower to forgo the elation of speed and freedom and bring the dogs to a halt. We broke out food and enjoyed lunch—or supper!

We camped that night on the upper reaches of Montana Creek. The next morning I left ahead of the dog team and, as I approached the fringes of timberline, ran into a flock of ptarmigan. They kept flying ahead as I walked up the trail, and when the dog team caught up with me, the ptarmigan accelerated their flight patterns, keeping in front of the dogs. As a result, the team gave John Semple a fast run up the final approaches to the pass at Henderson Dome. Not long afterwards Victor Henry caught up and walked past me and disappeared over the top of the divide. When I, too, finally reached the summit, I paused for a look around. Along the ridge to my left was Henderson Dome with billowy white clouds streaming overhead. I turned and looked to the north and saw the Indian River valley in the far distance, and behind the river, King Solomon's Dome from which most of the principal gold-bearing creeks of the Klondike emerge. Many a gold seeker was convinced that the "motherlode" would some day surely be found on that mountain—men like Sam Hafstead, who wandered the creeks around there for most of his life looking for it. He even left funds in his will to supply beer to the pallbearers who would lug his body up to the top of Haystack Mountain, a prominent hill in the area, so he could be buried near that motherlode. Geologists insist that there was never such a thing as a "motherlode" in that country, but even today prospectors ignore the geologists and continue to search the area.

A bitter wind was blowing through the pass, and I realized that the others had gone over the crest of the hill in order to avoid the wintry blasts that prevailed at that four-thousand-foot level. Sure enough, they had camped for lunch about two hundred yards down the trail, and after consuming sandwiches together we parted again. Vic Henry struck out ahead, followed by the dogs bounding down the steep trail with driver John Semple's foot riding the brake. If he could hold the team on this slope, he could hold them anywhere. I looked over the upper reaches of the left (north) fork of Henderson Creek to see if there were any identifiable landmarks, but other than a distant gap where the Yukon River wound its way through the hills, nothing was familiar. I was literally among the clouds, which whipped by me like a phalanx of ghosts touching here and there on the mountain in a whimsical dance.

As it reached timber, the trail suddenly broke into an even steeper descent, angling down into an ice-draped couloir that plunged thirty feet. I wondered how Semple had mastered this obstacle without the dog team and sled flying in all directions, but then he and Victor Henry knew their business, and I never saw either of them defeated by such hazards. After that, the trail levelled out and descended gradually, and we met few obstacles until the north fork widened and became deeper. Here I ran into a wide pocket of slush ice, and noticing that the team had backtracked and circled around this obstacle, I did the same. It was about a three-hour walk from the dome to the cabin, and I finally reached it at 2:30 p.m. The others had already pitched the tent next to the cabin, and we sat down for dinner and took it easy. The weather was mild.

The next day John Semple departed early to go back to Grand Forks and pick up Joe Henry and Eleanor Millard, a social worker who had volunteered to cook for the outfit. Victor Henry and I left camp on foot for Stewart River. The motor toboggans of the Langevin party had gone down the left fork for about four miles past the London cabin before they had turned around. This part of the trail was, therefore, well-packed but there was a three-mile gap of unbroken trail between that point and the end of the dogsled trail the Burians kept open all winter in order to tend their trapline on the right fork of Henderson Creek. If they had not run that line, I'm sure I would never have reached their place that night. Breaking trail in heavy snow is the most excruciating physical task I know of, and it took the two of us nine hours and twenty minutes to travel those eighteen miles. We took it easy all day Friday and enjoyed Yvonne Burian's servings of moose steak that were delectable beyond description, helping me to forget my aches and pains.

Robin Burian showed me the skin of a grizzly he had shot as the result of an odd incident the previous fall. He and his brother Ivan had been hunting when they spotted a bear sitting in a slough with its back to them. But the bear appeared to be preoccupied, and the way it was rocking back and forth indicated it was afloat! Robin could not figure out whether it was a black or a grizzly and kept switching bullets—more grains for a grizzly, fewer for a black bear. Finally, he took a lesser-grained bullet and killed the bear. It turned out to be a small grizzly that was rocking because it was sitting on top of two moose with locked horns. Robin figured the moose must have drowned while they were fighting, and he displayed their heads to us just as he had found them, locked in mortal combat. When the grizzly had stumbled onto this sudden dinner bonanza, it probably could not make up its mind on which moose to commence feasting. Consequently, the floating moose were rocking as the bear shifted from one to the other.

The next day when Victor Henry and I returned to the London cabin with Robin Burian and his team, it took us just a little over three hours. The dogs pulled steadily, setting a perfect pace, as they were in excellent shape from having been in harness all winter. Three of them were named after spirits of liquor. The leader was Rye, number two was Brandy and Gin was the wheel dog. Jack was number three and then came Teddy (who quit in '65) in the number four position. Rye and Brandy were sons of Scotty, Victor Henry's leader.

Later that afternoon Robin Burian and Victor Henry cut down another tree for ring-dating, while I walked up the trail to see if there was any sign that John Semple was coming back with Joe Henry and Eleanor Millard. When I met them about three miles above the cabin, Semple told me it had taken him only ten hours to drive the team the sixty miles into Dawson City from the cabin, demonstrating what a good team could do when it was in shape and running over a packed trail with no load but the driver. They went on to camp, and I waited to see if Joe Henry was following. He was seventy at the time, but knowing the physical condition he was in, it did not surprise me at all to see him appear around a bend in the trail about fifteen minutes behind the dog team. He had walked all the way from Quartz Creek, a distance of forty miles. Joe's son Victor contended there were few men young or old in the Yukon who could beat him in a long distance race in deep snow.

In the winter of 1928 Joe Henry had participated in a dramatic rescue to save the life of Reverend Richard Martin, who had gone hunting in the ring of mountains that surround the junction of the Blackstone and Ogilvie rivers about 170 miles north of Dawson City. Reverend Martin had lost the sight of his left eye in an accident in his youth and thus was in a vulnerable position if anything were to happen to his one good eye. On this occasion he took a shot at a caribou with his Ross rifle. The Ross, however, sometimes displayed a peculiar fault: the bolt failed to fix the cartridge in a firm position when rammed into the breech. In Martin's case, when the firing pin of the bolt hit the cartridge, it exploded and drove the bolt back into his good eye, puncturing it and driving it out of its socket.

Fortunately, Martin had been accompanied by his dog and now, unable to see and sick with pain, he called the animal to him and commanded him to lead him home. Martin's son Joe found them several miles from camp, and the elder Martin told him to mush to Joe Henry's camp for help. Young Joe sped eastward fifty miles to collect Joe Henry, who joined him with his team, and they raced back to Martin. Lashing the injured man to the sled, they headed for Dawson City. In an incredible ordeal, the two men mushed up the Blackstone River, through rugged Seela Pass, down the Chandindu River and then up the Yukon River to Dawson in four days. Martin was shipped out to Vancouver in the hope that his eye could be saved, but it was too late. He was never to see again. In 1969 he was almost ninety years old and living in the Dawson City hospital.

Joe and I continued down the trail to the London cabin, pausing briefly to glance at the remains of several cabins located about a mile above it and about a hundred yards off the trail. The next day we went back to these ruins and, using our snowshoes for shovels, scooped the snow out of the centre of the first cabin to discover a stone furnace. Judging by this heating unit, the cabin must have offered fairly primitive living conditions. In fact, Joe called it an "old-time" cabin, inferring that it predated the others along the creek including London's. We visited three more sites that had the unlived-in look of cabins hastily built by claim stakers and abandoned when hurriedly dug shafts proved up nothing more than barren bedrock.

However, in one sense the people who had once staked claims and panned for gold along Henderson's left fork were slightly different from those on most creeks scattered over the northland because they had been immortalized in Jack London's stories. His habit of using the real surnames of the people he had known was seldom employed by other authors, and I wondered if he had intended to forever record the names of those with whom he had shared his gold rush struggles. Most of these men had left, never to return. Some like Con Gepfert had gone home and ventured back. Others like Jim Goodman, Charlie Meyers and Fred Thompson stayed on a few years, but as far as I can ascertain the only individual close to London who remained in the Yukon Territory until his death was Louis Savard.

Researching the history of Henderson Creek had been at best a frustrating task that consumed hours snatched while I was engaged in other pursuits, and I was always grateful to get first-hand interviews to confirm the facts. If the historian waits until men are gone or memories are dim, much is lost as to the true nature of the events. Thus I found it most amazing that Jack London never composed an autobiographical sketch of his adventures in the Klondike. He may have figured he would destroy the aura of romance and mystery that enveloped his fiction if he wrote specifically about his own experiences, but when he died prematurely at the age of forty in 1916, he took with him the sources of his inspiration.

It was a sad occasion as Joe Henry and I poked around the old cabins, with the ghosts of the prototypes of Smoke Bellew, Burning Daylight, White Fang and Buck to haunt us, because we knew that almost all of London's colleagues were gone. "Come on," I said at last, "let's go back to camp. Maybe we can come back here next summer and dig around a bit."

We spent almost a week wandering through the creeks, Joe Henry hunting caribou, his son and John Semple trapping rabbits and hunting, and Eleanor Millard doing the cooking. Finally, it came time for her to return to Dawson City and for the Oakland group to fly into Stewart Island. While the two younger men hitched the dogs to the toboggan, I set out ahead of them and snowshoed down the trail toward the Yukon River. I had been on the trail about a half an hour when the dog team came trotting along sans Millard and Semple. Grasping the situation at a glance, I grabbed the sled and tipped it over, bringing the dogs to a halt. Obviously, when the sled was being loaded, the dogs had somehow broken away from their tether rope and headed down the trail alone. This situation has arisen more than once with veteran dog mushers. If a man is alone and his team gets away, it can run for many miles without stopping, and often when it does stop, the dogs get to fighting and serious injuries can result. When the others caught up, since we were not carrying supplies, I climbed aboard with Millard and rode for most of the journey. The only time we got off was when we came to steep banks.

On Tuesday, April 8, the Oakland party flew in and landed in a ski-equipped Great Northern Airways Beaver. Barry Watson, bush pilot for the company, put the plane down like a feather on the Yukon River across from the Burian home, and Rudy, Robin, Eleanor Millard and I went out to meet the new arrivals. Eddie Albert, the famous stage and screen star noted for his shock of blond hair and friendly smile, was the first one out. He remarked on the beauty of the country, and then after a picture-taking session, climbed onto the sled that Rudy Burian had waiting for him and they mushed back to the Burian home. Russ Kingman, the ebullient advertising man who was responsible for putting through the California part of the project, turned out to be a dog lover, so he was really in his element with no fewer than seventeen dogs to befriend during the expedition. Fred Reicker, the director of public relations for the Port of Oakland, was followed out of the plane by blond Jack Williamson, whose services Reicker had obtained as cinematographer for the expedition. Last off was Sergeant Ralph Godfrey of the Oakland

Police Department. At six feet four, he was the tallest member of the expedition. He had been employed to compare the signature on the slab with exemplars of London's handwriting, and his main purpose for coming on the trip was to see if the slab fit the slash on the wall of the cabin. He would also examine the structure closely to see if there were any clues to give additional proof of the cabin's authenticity. The men lined up for photographs with pilot Barry Watson, then a few walked and some rode by dog team across the river to the Burians' home.

The next morning Sergeant Godfrey, Fred Reicker and I set off on foot a good two hours ahead of the dog teams. We followed the path that cut diagonally across Upper Island, over Henderson Slough and then hiked up to where the trail climbed a bench on the north side of Henderson Creek. The trail was by now solid and hard, much like walking on a sidewalk. Though we made good time, the dog teams caught up with us quickly. We had put together three teams to take the Oakland group to the cabin and had arranged to trade places so everyone got a chance to ride. However, since Kingman wanted to make sure that Williamson took the proper film shots of Eddie Albert on the trail, John Semple's team began the trip carrying Eddie Albert, Rudy Burian's took Jack Williamson and Robin Burian's toted Russ Kingman. When they caught up to us, we took a short break while Jack Williamson shot 16 mm movie footage of the teams and men.

After only a short ride, Russ Kingman disembarked from his sled and was replaced by Fred Reicker so the latter could take photos of the dog teams farther up the creek. Godfrey, Kingman and I then continued up the trail. The path was picturesque as it meandered through groves of spruce—except in the immediate vicinity of the forks, an area that had been described in London's short story "To Build a Fire." I pointed the forks out to Kingman and Godfrey, but like so many places we visualize, the immediate area—being a jungle of willows—was a disappointment to them. I assured them that in summer the junction is much more appealing. London wrote:

> He held on through the level stretch of woods for several miles, crossed a wide flat, and dropped down a bank to the frozen bed of a small stream. This was Henderson Creek, and he knew he was ten miles from the forks. He looked at his watch. It was ten o'clock. He was making four miles an hour, and he calculated that he would arrive at the forks at half-past twelve. He decided to celebrate that event by eating his lunch there.

The central character in this story reaches the forks at twelve-thirty, has lunch and then walks for another hour up the left fork of the creek. About four miles from the fork he stumbles into overflow, freezes his hands and feet, and then dies on the trail. But when I took a closer look at London's estimates of distance and time, I realized that they did not correlate with the reality. He stated it was ten miles to the forks of the creek and the character in his story was walking about four miles an hour. Plainly, London was measuring the man's hike from his own cabin on Stewart Island to the forks. And earlier in the story he estimated that the man would reach camp "where the boys were already" on the left fork of Henderson at about 6:00 p.m. However, if he was making four miles an hour, it would put that camp over the summit of Henderson Dome, outside the Henderson watershed altogether.

Dog team travel is not without its hazards, and riding as a passenger can be similar to riding a bucking bronco because the passenger has to get the hang of swaying with the movement of the sled. Unfortunately for Eddie Albert, when John Semple

Oaklanders and Yukoners at the cabin. Front row, left to right: Rudy Burian, Vic Henry, Robin Burian. Back row: Jack Williamson, Ralph Godfrey, John Semple, Dick North, actor Eddie Albert, Joe Henry and Russ Kingman. *Russ Kingman*

drove his dogs down a creek bank and they could not make the turn, his sled tipped over and Albert spun off it into the snow.

We had a few chuckles when Russ Kingman sang out, "Hold that pose right there, Eddie. This is the photo I've been waiting for."

Halfway up the creek Reicker, Godfrey and I climbed aboard the sleds while the others, including Eddie Albert, walked. When asked how he was enjoying the trip, he replied, "Quite a ride, quite a ride. It is an unusual experience. Those dogs don't have any middle gears though. It's either all out at the beginning or not at all." When dogs start out they run as fast as they can, and the only thing that slows them to a sensible gait is their own tiredness. On this day as the three teams were in tremendous

During a lunch of moose meat sandwiches, actor Eddie Albert enter-
tains by catching the salt. *Russ Kingman*

shape, the entire party had reached the cabin by eleven o'clock.

The Oaklanders could not get enough of the atmosphere of
the dog teams, the creek and the old cabin that they now saw
for the first time. Though unchanged in seventy years, it was
the worse for wear, but it was there and it represented a man
whose fame was worldwide and whose writings about the creek
were translated into countless languages including Esperanto,
Macedonian, Greek, Turkish, Bengali, Japanese, Chinese and
Vietnamese. The world had come to know this creek through
London's writings, yet very few people in the world or even the
Yukon had ever set foot on the left fork of Henderson Creek.
Even today in the Yukon Territory there are only a handful of
people who have ever walked along the banks of Henderson's
left fork.

We ate a lunch consisting of moose meat sandwiches and

then began taking pictures of the cabin from all angles. Godfrey snooped around the cabin a bit, carefully studying the handwriting on the front door, the same writing that I had not paid much attention to on my first visit to the cabin. It turned out there was more to it than I had supposed, for it actually read: *February 26, 1915, Going to Dawson–Floyd Miles.* On the previous visit

"It fits!" Ralph Godfrey fits the slab to the slash. *Russ Kingman*

I'd misread the date as 1945 and the word "miles" in relation to a distance.

Next Godfrey took from his pack the slab that had been hacked out of the cabin so many years before by Jack MacKenzie. Here again was another crucial step in the restoration process. Would the slab fit the old slash on the log? If it doesn't, I thought, I'll slap on my snowshoes, head up the creek and keep going. I watched as the police sergeant patiently unwrapped it, and I saw the hole in it where it had been lifted off a knot. Sure enough, the knot was still on the log. He slipped the slab over the knot and it fit perfectly. The last step in that long journey which had commenced so many years before was completed. Eddie Albert broke out a bottle of Loomis wine, and we drank a toast to the success of the project.

Meanwhile, all day the temperature had been climbing steadily from below the zero mark to well above freezing. We were in a chinook—one of the warm winds that occasionally blanket the northern forests, turning snow into slop. Consequently, all the time we were examining the cabin those of us who lived in the north had been looking anxiously at the sky. Sloppy snow was bad enough, but if we were hit with a rain squall we would really be in trouble as there might be considerable difficulty crossing streams. As well, in many places the snow might be washed away, leaving nothing but barren muskeg, and the dogs were tired enough without the added burden of having to pull a sled over snowless ground. But that was the Yukon for you. It always seemed to have a trick to pull on the unwary. The man who became complacent in such a vast wilderness was asking for trouble.

We discussed the situation. Robin and Rudy Burian said they would need to give the dogs a bit more rest, and I suggested that we stay the night and hope for a drop of temperature in the morning.

"What if it doesn't drop?" Albert asked. He explained he had other obligations and really did not have time to linger, as much as he wanted to.

It was finally decided that we would go back that same day. The others from Oakland were game, though they did not realize how rugged eighteen miles in soft snow could be. The stage was set for a true-life adventure that would have keenly interested Jack London himself.

The dog teams stayed behind to rest a little longer while we started off on foot with Eddie Albert and Joe Henry leading the way. Joe had his snowshoes with him as did I. The others were without: they had not been needed as in the morning the ground had been frozen. Fortunately the trail was still easily visible, though already fast melting away in some locations, but if darkness descended while we were on the trail the men would have to stay alert or they would find themselves wandering aimlessly through the bush. A sudden plunge in temperature then could cause trouble.

In less than an hour we were spread over miles of trail. Though used to hiking in the bush by this time, I found every step an excruciating struggle because of the shin-deep slush. Sweat poured off my brow and in a short time my underclothes were soaked with perspiration, and I knew the others must be suffering equally as they pushed down the trail. Big men suffer more than slight men at such times because a light man can travel on top of a crust where a heavy man will crash through it. Ralph Godfrey stood six feet four and burdened by clothes that protected him at thirty degrees below zero but were too heavy for the warmth of the chinook, he began to falter after we had only gone five miles. Besides, he had already walked twelve miles in the morning.

"Go ahead, Dick," he said, "I'll just follow along."

But you travel in pairs at all times in the Yukon if it is

possible, and as the others had surged ahead I stayed with him, worrying about the strain he was under as he struggled through the wet, sloppy snow. I knew he was almost as old as Eddie Albert, who was sixty, and had been spending most of his time at a desk, which is definitely no place to get in training for a hike of this kind. I had another worry: his pace was very slow, it was getting toward dark and we were not even halfway to the Burians' home. Finally, I hurried ahead to confer with Russ Kingman, Fred Reicker and Jack Williamson, who had decided to wait for us. Eddie Albert and Joe Henry were out of sight down the trail. Though the oldest, they were probably in better shape than all the rest of us.

We decided I would stay with Godfrey and that Kingman, who was a good hiker, would go on. If we needed help, he would get it. Jack Williamson decided to accompany Kingman, and Fred Reicker volunteered to stay with me in case Godfrey's condition worsened. Finally, however, the dog teams came down the trail, though it was a tremendous struggle for them as well, as this warm air was the worst sort of condition for working dogs. They were panting heavily and almost played out, yet we agreed Godfrey would have to be given a ride part of the way. We dumped a portion of the load off one sled and the police sergeant scrambled aboard, then the sleds and men left us and headed down the trail. Fred Reicker and I plodded after them.

An hour or so later, we were surprised to come across Godfrey again. It seems the dog teams had caught up with Eddie Albert and Joe Henry. By this time the sun had gone down and the temperature was rapidly falling off. Though Albert had walked fifteen miles and was still going strong, his feet were soaked and there was a possibility they would freeze. On learning this, Godfrey suddenly got off his sled and offered his place to Albert, explaining that he was wearing appropriate footgear—snow packs—which Albert did not have. Not knowing Godfrey's condition, Albert got aboard the sled and the teams went on, leaving Godfrey, Williamson, Reicker, Kingman and me behind.

We walked on. The darkness now enveloped us like a black shroud. The eerie howl of a timber wolf suddenly broke the silence and reverberated through the lonely forest. Then another sounded and still another. It was scary but better to hear them than suffer the incredible "white silence" of the northern wilderness.

Godfrey fought his way gamely down the trail, but now he could go only forty or fifty yards at a time. "Go on, I'll catch up," he said at one point as he lay down beneath a large spruce tree. "I'll take a little nap and be okay." It sounded too much like London's short story, "To Build a Fire." To lie down in that country in winter was courting death. We let him rest for a while, then he struggled to his feet and went forward for several hundred more yards. He was walking on sheer grit.

Now the temperature was dropping fast. The Yukon is like that: a seventy-degree dip in temperature in a day is not an uncommon occurrence. During our trip the temperature varied from thirty below zero at sunrise to forty above in mid-afternoon. Almost on that exact same day, the sudden warm spell lured a man to his death on the Top of the World Highway that connects the Alaska Highway with Dawson City. He had set out to walk from Jack Wade Creek in Alaska to the Clinton Creek Asbestos Mine in the Yukon. When the temperature dropped, he froze to death about halfway to his goal. Several weeks later his body was found in a snowdrift just off the road.

Knowing the dog teams would have to get rested before heading back for us, we took a break and then plunged on. In the meantime, Kingman and Williamson, having gained a couple of miles on us, reached the flats of Henderson Slough and suddenly lost the trail in the darkness. Now Williamson, who had probably travelled twice the distance of the rest of us as he ran back and forth shooting films of the trip, also became played out and told Kingman to go on. He said he would catch a catnap and then follow, but Kingman told him that if he did he might never wake up again.

"The Burians' place is around the next bend," Kingman said, though he judged they had four more back-breaking miles to go. First, however, they had to find the trail again, and he didn't know if they were to the left or right of it. They had also heard the wolves howling, and though they realized wolves seldom attack a man, there was always room for doubt.

Jack Williamson observed, "Hell, Russ, if dogs will attack a man, why wouldn't wolves?"

Kingman admitted he had no answer for that question, and he began circling their stopping point searching for the trail. He missed it and tried again, this time making a wider circle. It was tough going through the thick buck brush and willows, but the northern lights were flickering across the sky, giving him a little light to go by, and he finally located the path. Williamson then got to his feet and the two men walked forward in the darkness with Kingman urging his partner to try for the next bend in the trail.

"It's only a little farther, Jack," he said.

They stopped for another break and Williamson cracked, "I wish I had two steaming cups of coffee."

"Yes, I know how you feel. Me too," Kingman said.

"Yeah," said Williamson, "I'd pour one in each boot."

Finally, after walking for ten straight hours, they saw the welcome twinkle of lights at the Burian home. They staggered through the doorway and were immediately supplied with hot coffee by Yvonne Burian.

"Where are the others?" Eddie Albert asked.

"Out on the trail," Kingman said. "Ralph's pretty tuckered out, though he should be okay once he gets in."

Albert shook his head in disgust. "If he had told me, I wouldn't have taken his place on the sled." Of course, if he had gone on walking, he might have lost a couple of toes. "You think we could get the dogs out again?" he asked Rudy Burian.

"Sure," he replied, "they should be rested up enough for a short trip. I imagine by now the others have reached the flats."

In fact, at this point we were still about three miles out. I was tired, but I had the advantage of wearing snowshoes. I had offered the use of them to my comrades, but as they had never worn them before, they figured the webbed shoes would be counter-productive. Reicker, however, was in excellent condition, and though it was a struggle he was evidently enjoying himself. Godfrey was now propelling himself along by willpower alone, and I had to admire his reservoir of strength.

When we had been on the trail for twelve straight hours (not counting the hike up to the cabin that morning), Reicker said he thought he saw a light. Neither Godfrey nor I could see it, and I figured Reicker might have caught sight of a star through the branches of the spruce trees that overlooked the trail. Then we did see it—a white spot bouncing through the darkness of the trees. Robin Burian and John Semple were driving two dog teams, and Robin was using a flashlight to avoid the tree branches. The dogs, of course, followed the trail with ease whether it was day or night or even if it was covered with a foot of new fallen snow. Their noses did not lie.

Fortunately, Robin had brought a thermos of hot tea and rum, and we agreed that it was the best drink we had ever tasted. Then with flashlights to illuminate the way, the teams took us on a wild night ride through the darkened forest. It was quite a sensation.

Our party assembled in the Burians' kitchen to recap the day's experiences, and Fred Reicker probably summed it up as well as anyone could have when he said, "I would have to say that this was the greatest trip of my life. There is something about travelling by dog team. Maybe it's the thrill when you barrel down a hill at fifteen miles an hour or the exhilaration of the arctic air clearing your lungs or of seeing a moose stumble from his bed as you mush by. I suppose if the word ever got out about what great fun this is, the Yukon would be overrun by winter tourists."

The next day we flew to Dawson City, where Mayor James Mellor and the city council held a public reception for the group. Hosts and guests made speeches, and then the Yukoners broke up into small groups to chat with the visitors. The project represented cooperation between the Yukon Territory and California, or more particularly Dawson City and Oakland, and it was a success mainly because of this cooperation. The Oakland group thanked the hosts for their hospitality and the next day flew to Whitehorse via Great Northern Airways and then by Canadian Pacific Airlines to Vancouver and on to California.

Eventually, Ralph Godfrey completed his study of the handwriting. He contended there were too many "unexplainable differences" for him to say the London writing was authentic. The pencilled writing on the vertical wood surface was the problem. There were no exemplars to compare with it. But acknowledging he was not a licensed examiner, he suggested I should find one. In turn, I asked the chief of the Alaska State Troopers fingerprint department, Robert LaPointe, to recommend a qualified man. He recommended Ludlow Baynard, who was licensed, taught the subject, and held the rank of captain in the Louisiana State Police. Baynard's report was affirmative with some reservations. He wrote:

I am of the opinion that the writing on the slash of white spruce was written by the same person (Jack London) on whose known exhibits I have made an analysis. It is also my opinion that the writer was not holding the writing instrument in the normal position, and had to be standing as the questioned writing was five feet above the ground level. The writing is also abnormally large.

I am of the opinion that the writer had gloves on or had his hand wrapped. Observations of the similarities in the questioned writing to the known writing tend to support this analysis, that the questioned writing is authentic, with some counter arguments. Because I have no reference material, I have been unable to account for many of the unknown factors, i.e.; writing on wood that has such a grain appearing on the surface.

Baynard added later that London may have held the pencil as one would a paint brush when he wrote his name. In other words, the writing instrument would have been held between his thumb and forefinger with the latter digit extended full length along the pencil. He then switched to the normal method for the rest of the inscription. The awkwardness of both approaches would explain the differences.

Robin Burian works on duplicate cabins at Stewart River (photographed with lead dog Rye and one of his pups). The cabin on the right
used the lower logs from the original and went to Dawson City. The
cabin on the left used the upper logs and went to Oakland, California.

10: TWIN CABINS BUILT AND MOVED

A few days after the Oakland group left, Rudy and Robin Burian drove their little International tractor from Stewart Island to the cabin, stopping in several places to fill deep fissures with snow in order to drive the tractor across the creek. They took the cabin apart log by log, making sure not to break the dovetail ends, and carefully wrapped the knot-in-the-slash with burlap before loading the host log onto the giant work-sled they had towed to the cabin site. The logs, all worth keeping, were numbered so there would be no trouble sorting them when the two cabins were built. They were also cautious with the window and door frames that had been attached to the logs by wooden pegs, and they draped the door with a tarp to protect the handwriting on it. All of the roof logs had to be discarded because they had rotted and the spruce pole bunks were also left behind.

Once the job of loading was completed, they cranked up the tractor and headed down the creek with the dismembered cabin in tow. The trip was not without its problems because the steep banks of the creek were not much easier navigating by tractor than they were by dog team. More than once, Jack London's cabin almost ended up in the creek, which was swollen with fast-thawing snow. And the structure almost disappeared altogether when they drove the load across the ice of Henderson Slough.

"The ice was groaning behind us," Robin said later.

Once back at Stewart Island, the Burians commenced the real work. By cutting down some spruce trees and salvaging logs from the broken-down roadhouse at the forks, they built two cabins. (Coincidentally, this was the same roadhouse where Jack London reputedly wrote a poem on the door.) There were forty-eight logs in the original cabin, thus twenty-four for each replica. That meant the Burians would have to come up with forty-eight more logs to create cabins of the exact same measurements as the original. This was not as easy as one might think as each one of the newly added logs would have to be hewn to match the original. This meant using a broad axe, which has a blade ideally fashioned for hewing or squaring logs.

One day Robin Burian deserted the cabin job in order to pick me up in Dawson City, and it was on this trip that the two of us miraculously avoided the exploding ice jam mentioned at the beginning of this book. Back at the house, he handed me a broad axe to get the feel of what it was like to hew a few logs. However, after observing my dexterity with the axe, he suggested it might be in my best interest to place one of my feet in a basket. Wielded by a neophyte, the wide axe blade has a tendency to glance off the log with attendant injury to one's foot. A basket, he said, might prevent damage.

His father told me he believed the cabin logs were actually hewn with a regular axe by the individual or individuals who put up the cabin. So, using implements other than axes to a refined degree, the father and son were going to the utmost lengths to recreate the cabins exactly the way the original was built. This included fashioning the interior fixtures such as the spruce pole bunks, a table, the door, and shelves. The door latch and door handle were hand-carved. However, they did not recreate some items because of their tendency to erode in the short term, though they probably could have. These included the moose-hide hinges that held up the door in the original shack.

Not long after my visit, the structures were completed with the logs being numbered again to facilitate fitting them back together. Then they were dismantled and transported by Rudy and Ivan Burian in their freight boat seventy-five miles down-river to Dawson City. This took four trips. One of the cabins was destined for a lot provided by the city near the Robert Service cabin, and it was rebuilt there by Rudy Burian with help from William DeWolfe, whose father had carried the mail by horse and dog team between Dawson City and the town of Eagle, Alaska, for many years. The senior DeWolfe won fame for his dependability and was known by stampeders as the "Iron Man of the Yukon." Others who helped by putting sod on the roof were Vince Frazer, Gary Langevin and the Anderson brothers.

The cabin destined for Oakland, California, was loaded onto a Klondike Express truck and dispatched to Whitehorse with expenses covered by the truck company's president Roy McDiarmid. He came close to losing both cabin and truck on their way south, however, when they were almost caught up in a huge forest fire that swept through the Pelly Crossing area. When the truck reached Whitehorse, Robin Burian, Joe Henry and I transferred the load to a second-hand, two-ton truck that my prospector friend Charlie Benson had acquired for us. Planning ahead, I had contacted Diane Murphy and Mike Miller of the Alaska Department of Tourism, and they had kindly furnished us with a pass by which we could travel to Seattle over the state marine highway system.

On June 15, 1969, the three of us set off in our truck, driving all night and arriving at the customs station at Haines the next day. The customs officer, Roy Cummerford, met us there, and we climbed down from the truck and followed him into the station. His questions were routine until he asked what we were carrying.

"Jack London's cabin," I said.

"You sure you don't have the northern lights on there instead?" he said wryly.

"No, honest," I replied. "It's an artifact or something." I really did not know what to call the cabin to a customs agent.

He glanced at the truck and scratched his head. "Let's see how we enter this." He thumbed through the customs regulations, looking for the section covering what we had aboard our truck, then threw up his hands in frustration. "Jack London's cabin!" he mumbled. "By gawd, I'm going to retire!" Finally he looked up at us and bellowed, "You're cleared."

We did not wait for him to change his mind. We putt-putted our old truck to the dock in Haines and boarded the motor vessel *Matanuska,* named for one of Alaska's great glaciers. Our ship set sail, stopping briefly at Juneau and at Ketchikan where we visited bewhiskered Lou Williams, publisher of the *Ketchikan Daily News,* who promised to print a publicity blurb about the cabin. While in port we also went up to the ship's bridge and visited briefly with the vessel's captain, Robert Smith. He had once run a tank landing ship along the Arctic coast supplying the outposts of the early warning network set up during the Cold War. Since Joe Henry had at one time been the skipper of the riverboat *Brainstorm,* which ran to Old Crow via the Yukon and Porcupine rivers, he was right at home on the bridge. The pilot's commands as we left the harbour brought back memories for Joe: "Let her go aft. Let her go forward. Left 20. Midships." And later, "Left 20, Steady 135...136. Five left. Give 10 left. Down five. Midships. Five left. Midships." I found myself thinking that a former seaman like Jack London would have enjoyed the action of the old pilot as he rattled off the orders and the able-bodied seaman called them back and responded with the wheel.

As our ship wound its way south via the historic inland passage through which London and his pals had travelled north aboard the *City of Topeka*, I was transfixed by the awesome majesty of the scenery. Towering, glacier-capped peaks in the background, infinite coniferous forests at their feet, and in the foreground seagulls, eagles and ravens overhead and killer whales and porpoises below. Fishing boats, rugged loggers' rafts, intrepid freighters and tankers rounded out the traffic—all of which was appealing to the eye. I understood why men went north and how that lure could seep into a man's bones and forever tug on him to return. It was easy to comprehend how "northern writers" like Jack London, Rex Beach, Robert Service, Pierre Berton and James Oliver Curwood could never really escape the influence of their northern experiences. No man with feeling could completely abandon such an umbrella. And though all of them eventually went to warmer climes, some of the happiest days of their lives were spent on the trail in the subarctic wilderness.

We disembarked in Seattle on June 20 and began our trip south. In Oregon we were stopped by a state trooper who asked for some sort of document or bill of lading for our load. We looked at him and at each other and shrugged. We hadn't the slightest idea what he was talking about. Resolutely he took out his pad and walked around to the front of the truck to write down the licence number. That was when he noticed the word "Yukon" on the plates, and smiling over the futility of life, he told us to "Get lost!" We thanked him profusely and I noted to my fellow travellers that there were obviously some advantages to being uninformed!

We drove on with Robin Burian at the wheel, me navigating and Joe Henry commenting on the scenery. At one point we went through a long tunnel and Joe said, "White man like gopher. Drive hole right through mountain." Another time we saw a large houseboat. "*Unchit* have house on water. Pretty good," Joe exclaimed.

Neither Joe nor Robin had ever been out in "civilization" before. In fact, the first traffic light either of them had ever seen was Whitehorse's one and only. And to this day I do not know if Robin even had a driver's licence. I was scared to ask. He drove well, however, and took a load off my shoulders as a result.

Our next crisis arose in the vicinity of Orinda, California, a town not far from Oakland where we stopped for gas. I had no credit card, but I did have a Canadian one-hundred-dollar bill, so before ordering the gas, I asked if they would change the bill.

The gas jockey looked at the bill like a hillbilly who could not read. "What's this?" he asked.

"Canajun hundred," I said.

"No dice!" he said. "We only take US."

It didn't take me long to find out that cashing Canadian currency in the lower United States was like Butch Cassidy trying to pass a personal cheque with the Union Pacific Railroad. This instrument would not fly. Ultimately, a kindly gent who ran the Orinda liquor store took pity on us, converted our one-hundred-dollar bill into US money, and we bought gas.

We pulled into the Jack London Inn at Jack London Square on June 22. It was not long before Russ Kingman arrived to take us to the office of Fred Reicker in Oakland's Port Authority building, and thus began a round of festivities. We were offered tickets to just about every sports event and show in the Bay area.

However, our first priority was to rebuild the cabin. The representatives of the Port said that since they had not yet ascertained exactly where they wanted to place the cabin in the square, it would be best for us to do the job in a nearby warehouse. Later they would bring it out with appropriate ceremonies. Robin's numbering system made the whole process of rebuilding the cabin quite easy, and we even received assistance

Left to right: Joe Henry with a pair of snowshoes he donated, Robin Burian and Dick North. *Wilson photo, Oakland Tribune*

from passerby Bill Rita, who suggested we "age" the fresh logs by applying a solution of linseed oil, lampblack, umber and turpentine. When I asked where he had learned the technique he replied, "The antique business."

We furnished the interior with items that would have been used by London and his pals in 1897. These included a Yukon stove, two caribou skins placed on the spruce pole bunks, a bearskin coat, hand-carved tables and stools, pick and shovel, axe, miner's candle holders, several gold pans, mooseskin boxes, a bearskin, a foxskin, several traps of the single-spring and double-spring variety, caps, mukluks, tin plates and kitchen utensils, wood pelt stretchers, a huge moosehorn over the door, two nineteenth-century bottles, an old-style griddle, pot dipper, square nails, Yukon flag, a valuable copper pot, an Indian dance jacket and a wood bucket. Once that task was completed we were free to enjoy the great hospitality of our hosts, which included several appearances before the news media including the David Niles radio show in San Francisco.

Both my companions were candid in their observations— maybe too candid. For example, Oakland's Channel 2 host Andrea Boggs, after hearing that Robin had never seen TV before, asked him what he thought of it.

Robin paused for a second and then said, "It's just as bad as I've read, maybe a little worse!"

Joe, who took to the David Niles radio show in San Francisco like iron pyrite does to a magnet said, "Dick, when are we going to Hollywood?"

But all in all, both men—who had in a sense suddenly surfaced amidst twentieth century technology—passed through it all with a marvellous degree of equanimity.

Thanks to Nancy Campbell, who served as both host and chauffeur for us, and to Russ and Winnie Kingman, we visited many places of interest, but the highlight was tea with the

Shepards at the Jack London estate. London's stepsister Eliza, who had married J.H. "Cap" Shepard, had supervised the ranch for London and was probably one of the few during his lifetime who managed his properties in an accountable manner. This propensity for effective management also carried over to her son Irving Shepard and to *his* son Milo Shepard, who manages the estate today. We were suitably impressed by viewing London's study and the bedroom in which the writer passed away, but to me it seemed too ironic that a man of such consummate energy, one so endowed with the spirit of adventure, would die in bed. Somehow you did not expect that of Jack London.

Irving Shepard filled us in on two of London's Klondike associates. He said that Fred Thompson, the diary keeper, had returned to California and resumed his old job as a court reporter in Santa Rosa. Later he moved to Sacramento, where his brother Rolfe was associate justice of the state Supreme Court. Another London associate, Del Bishop, dropped by occasionally to say hello to London and later to the Shepards, and Irving recalled Bishop talking about going to Siberia on a gold rush early in the 1900s. Bishop also said that before the Klondike rush he had been one of the discoverers of the famous Monte Cristo property in northwest Washington state, a mine that was later purchased by H.G. Bond whose sons Louis and Marshall had worked it for a short time before embarking for the Klondike in 1897.

Irving Shepard was a friendly, deliberate man, and the most knowledgeable person then alive with respect to the personality of his uncle, Jack London. This was quite obviously due to the fact that he had been raised in the great author's shadow. As he was aware of the restoration of the Jack London cabin, I felt it was incumbent to solicit his opinion on the signature and produced an enlargement for him to see. He scanned it carefully, noted some differences, then looked up and said, "In close detail there are differences, but they can be easily dismissed due to the

vertical surface. Overall, my impression is that the inscription was written by my uncle." Shepard's wife, however, would not dismiss the details so easily. She did not think it was London's handwriting. But differences of opinion make horse races, and I guess we will never be absolutely certain it is London's signature without him around to confirm it.

But it is the cabin itself that embodies the spirit of Jack London. It was his refuge, his sanctuary, the place where he could obtain a maximum of warmth with a minimum of fuel. And it played a focal part in many of his stories. It is a symbol of a more simplistic era but not so far removed from us that we can ignore the fact that some day we may be forced to return to the same kind of humble dwelling in order to survive.

Opposite page, Twin cabins in their permanent locations: top, Dawson City, Yukon; below, Oakland, California.

EPILOGUE: THE PAPER TRAIL

The years have flown by since the cabins were completed and moved to their respective sites in Oakland and Dawson City, but the research projects initiated during that time left me with a fascinating collection of photographs and documents gathering dust in a closet. One day in 1985 my wife said, "Why don't you do something with that paper trail?"

"Like what?" I asked.

"Put it on exhibit or something like that," she replied.

So with a display in mind, I wrote to Chuck Holloway, general manager of the Klondike Visitors Association (KVA) in Dawson City, a non-profit operation that promotes tourism. It is funded by the profits from Diamond Tooth Gertie's Gambling Hall, one of the first casinos approved in Canada. In my letter I explained that I wanted to set up an in-depth photo and document display that would highlight London's life and his fiction as it related to the Yukon Territory and Alaska. Holloway could see the tourism potential and after suggesting a trial run for one summer, he submitted my proposal to the KVA's board. They approved it in 1986 and after passing the test that summer the collection went on permanent display in 1987 in a log exhibit hall built at the cabin site specifically to house my collection. It was funded by the KVA and the territorial and federal governments.

BIBLIOGRAPHY

A-No 1 (Leon Ray Livingston). *From Coast to Coast with Jack London*. Erie, PA: The A-No 1 Publishing Company, 1917. Reprinted 1969, Grand Rapids, MI: Black Letter Press.

Adney, Tappan. *The Klondike Stampede*. New York: Harper, 1900.

Bond, Marshall Jr. *Gold Hunter: The Adventures of Marshall Bond*. Albuquerque: University of New Mexico Press, 1969.

Clifford, Howard. *The Skagway Story*. Anchorage, Alaska: Alaska Northwest Publishing Co., 1983.

Cole, Terrence. *E.T. Barnette*. Anchorage, Alaska: Alaska Northwest Publishing Co., 1981.

Coutts, Robert C. *Yukon: Places and Names*. Sidney, British Columbia: Gray's Publishing Ltd., 1980.

DeArmond, Robert N. *Early Visitors to Southeastern Alaska*. Alaska Northwest Publishing Co., 1978.

DeArmond, Robert N. *The Founding of Juneau*. Juneau, Alaska: Gastineau Channel Centennial Association, 1980.

Denison, Merrill. *Klondike Mike*. New York: William Morrow & Co., 1943.

Hamilton, David M. *The Tools of My Trade: The Annotated Books in Jack London's Library*. Seattle: University of Washington Press, 1986.

Hendricks, King, and Irving Shepard, eds. *Letters from Jack London*. New York: Odyssey, 1965.

Jonas, Shirley. *Ghosts of the Klondike*. Skagway, Alaska: Lynn Canal Publishing Co., 1993.

King, Jean Beach. *Arizona Charlie*. Phoenix: Heritage Publishers, 1989.

Kingman, Russ. *A Pictorial Life of Jack London*. New York: Crown Publishers, 1979.

_____. *Jack London: A Definitive Chronology*. Middletown, California: David Rejl, 1992.

Labor, Earl, Robert C. Leitz III, and I. Milo Shepard, eds. *The Complete Short Stories of Jack London*. Three volumes. Palo Alto, California: Stanford University Press, 1993.

Labor, Earl, Robert C. Leitz III, and I. Milo Shepard, eds. *The Letters of Jack London*. Three volumes. Palo Alto, California: Stanford University Press, 1988.

Labor, Earl and Jeanne Campbell Reesman. *Jack London*. Revised edition. New York: Twayne Publishers, 1994.

London, Charmian Kittredge. *The Book of Jack London*. Two volumes. New York: The Century Co., 1921.

London, Jack. *Burning Daylight*. New York: Macmillan, 1919.

_____. *The Call of the Wild*. New York: Macmillan, 1903.

_____. *Children of the Frost*. New York: Macmillan, 1902.

_____. *A Daughter of the Snows*. Philadelphia: J.B. Lippincott Co., 1902.

_____. *The Faith of Men*. New York: Macmillan, 1904.

_____. *The God of His Fathers*. New York: McClure, Phillips and Co., 1901.

_____. *John Barleycorn*. New York: The Century Co., 1913. Reprinted by Oxford University Press, 1998.

_____. *Lost Face*. New York: Macmillan, 1910.

_____. *Love of Life*. New York: Macmillan, 1907.

_____. *Smoke Bellew*. New York: The Century Co., 1912.

_____. *The Son of the Wolf*. Boston: Houghton Mifflin, 1900.

_____. *White Fang*. New York: Macmillan, 1906.

London, Joan. *Jack London and His Times*. New York: Doubleday, Doran, 1939; rpt Seattle: University of Washington Press, 1968.

Mayo Historical Society. *Gold & Galena: a History of the Mayo*

District. Compiled by Linda E.T. MacDonald and Lynette R. Bleiler. Mayo, Yukon: Mayo Historical Society, 1990.

North, Dick. *Arctic Exodus.* Toronto: Macmillan of Canada, 1991.

Satterfield, Archie. *Chilkoot Pass.* Revised and expanded edition. Anchorage, Alaska: Alaska Northwest Publishing, 1980.

Schwatka, Frederick. *A Summer in Alaska.* Philadelphia: John Y. Huber Co., 1891.

Sinclair, Andrew. *Jack: A Biography of Jack London.* New York: Harper and Rowe, 1977.

Sinclair, James M. *Mission Klondike.* Vancouver, British Columbia: Mitchell Press Ltd., 1978.

Sisson, James III, ed. *Jack London's Articles and Short Stories in the Aegis.* Oakland, California: Star Rover House, 1980.

Stone, Irving. *Sailor on Horseback.* Boston: Houghton Mifflin, 1938.

Walker, Franklin. *Jack London and the Klondike.* San Marino, California: Huntington Library, 1966.

Woodbridge, Hensley C., John London, and George Tweney, eds. *Jack London: A Bibliography.* Georgetown, California: Talisman Press, 1966.

INTERVIEWS AND CORRESPONDENCE

Ludlow B. Maynard, Examiner of Document, Baton Rouge, Louisiana. Letter: August 10, 1983.

H.E. Wahlgren, In-charge, Wood Quality Evaluation Research, Forest Products Lab, Madison, WN. Letter: June 1, 1970.

JIM GOODMAN'S RELATIVES:

Rex Kettlewell, nephew, Nampa, Idaho. Letters: March 19, 1982; August 9, 1982.

Billie (Ima) Knudson, niece, Santa Rosa, CA. Enclosure with her cousin Rex Kettlewell's letter.

Elizabeth Young McCutcheon, daughter-in-law of Jim Young, Goodman's cousin, Healdsburg, CA. Letters: December 2, 1981; June 16, 1982; July 26, 1982; November 16, 1983.

Betty Pierce, grandniece, Paradise, CA. Letter: December 9, 1983.

Ila Stains, Santa Rosa, CA. Interview.

Pearl Goodman Wood, grandniece, Chewelah, WN. Letters: December 10, 1983; May 27, 1984; February 25, 1985.

IRA MERRITT SLOPER'S RELATIVES:

Myra Kell McCreery, grandniece, Paso Robles, CA. Letter: June 23, 1993.

Loma Sloper Taylor, grandniece, Renton, WN. Letter: circa 1993.

MARTIN WILBORN TARWATER'S RELATIVES:

Mary Inglis Sims, grandniece, Sacramento, CA. Letter: November 21, 1981.

Francis Tarwater, grandson, Santa Rosa, CA. Letter: February 24, 1983.

NEWSPAPER SOURCES

Dawson City Daily News – Nov. 22, 1916

Dawson City News – Jan. 20, 1934

Klondike News – April 1, 1898

San Francisco Examiner – July 20, 25, 26, 31. Aug. 14, 21, 23, 1897

Santa Rosa Press Democrat – Nov. 10, 1916

Santa Rosa Republican – Sept. 28, 1932

Sitka Alaskan – June 19, Aug. 7, Aug. 23, 1897

INDEX

About the Author

Dick North is the author of several books including *The Mad Trapper of Rat River* and *The Lost Patrol*. North spent twenty years as the curator of the Jack London Interpretive Centre and Museum in Dawson City and is a member of the Jack London (Yukon) Society. North is the recipient of the Lifetime Achievement Award granted by the Yukon Historical and Museums Association in honour of his literary works in the historical field and was nominated for the Order of Canada in 2006. He currently lives in Dawson City, Yukon.